CW01655274

UK Financial Services

Compliance Manager's Guidebook & Reference

The 'Go To' Reference Book for All UK Financial Services Compliance & Risk Managers for the 2020's

Published by: Compliance Consultant

Author: Lee Werrell Chartered FCSI

--- * --- *** --- ***--- *** --- *** --- ***--- *** --- *** ---**

--- * --- *** --- ***--- *** --- *** --- ***--- *** --- *** ---**

Contents Table

Chapter 1: The Regulatory Environment in the UK Including PSD2

The financial services industry in the United Kingdom has undergone significant regulatory changes since the implementation of the Financial Services Act in 1988. The compliance function, once viewed as an unnecessary burden by many financial firms, has become an integral part of the regulatory landscape. This evolution stems from the industry's initial attempts at self-regulation, which, despite some successes in the City of London's broking sector, ultimately failed to prevent widespread exploitation of loopholes and grey areas by financial advisers, banks, and insurance companies. This led to customer detriment, confusion, and a general mistrust of financial institutions and their representatives

In response to these issues, a robust, coherent, and transparent regulatory framework was established, necessitating the creation of independent, well-resourced, and commercially aware compliance departments within financial firms. This framework aims to ensure consistent consumer outcomes across all sectors of the financial services industry, from small tax-free investments to corporate needs and investment banking.

While successive governments have been keen to oversee the financial services sector, it became apparent that they lacked sufficient resources to adequately monitor the diverse range of business models and types within the industry. Consequently, the compliance department emerged as an internal regulatory agent, funded and resourced proportionately to the size of the institution it represents. Although compliance functions now justify their existence in their own right, it is important to recognise that they remain an extension of the regulatory regime and can only be fully understood within the context of the UK's regulatory framework.

This book is not intended to replace the FCA Handbook, as it is evolving continuously, but intends to assist the UK Financial Services Compliance Director/Manager by providing practical help on a variety of subjects.

The UK Regulators

The regulatory landscape in the UK has evolved significantly over the years. Until 2013, the Financial Services Authority (FSA) was widely perceived as the sole financial regulator, operating under the Financial Services and Markets Act 2000 (FSMA). However, this was a simplistic view that did not accurately reflect the complexity of the regulatory environment.

In reality, numerous regulatory bodies oversaw various aspects of financial services activities in the UK. These included the Pensions Regulator, the Panel for Takeovers and Mergers (POTAM), and peripheral organisations such as the Office of Fair Trading (OFT) and the Information Commissioner's Office (ICO).

A New Regulatory Dawn

On 1 April 2013, a significant restructuring of financial regulation in the UK took place, known as the "legal cut-over". The FSA was split into two distinct regulatory bodies: the Prudential Regulation Authority (PRA) and the Financial Conduct Authority (FCA). Additionally, a third body, the Financial Policy Committee (FPC), was established within the Bank of England to provide guidance on matters of financial stability to both the PRA and FCA.

The current system for regulating financial services in the UK involves several bodies, each with specific responsibilities and objectives:

1. The Financial Conduct Authority (FCA)

The FCA is responsible for ensuring that relevant markets function well, supervising the conduct of financial services firms, and overseeing the prudential supervision of firms not supervised by the PRA. Its statutory objective is "to ensure that the relevant markets function well", supported by three operational objectives:

- To secure an appropriate degree of protection for consumers
- To protect and enhance the integrity of the UK financial system
- To promote effective competition in the interests of consumers

2. The Prudential Regulation Authority (PRA)

The PRA, a subsidiary of the Bank of England, is responsible for promoting the stable and prudent operation of the financial system through regulation of all deposit-taking institutions, insurers, and significant investment firms. Its statutory objectives are:

- To promote the safety and soundness of the firms it regulates
- Specifically for insurers, to contribute to securing an appropriate degree of protection for policyholders

3. The Bank of England

The Bank of England is responsible for protecting and enhancing the UK's financial stability. It has primary operational responsibility for financial crisis management and oversees payment systems, settlement systems, and clearing houses. The Bank is also the UK's resolution authority.

4. The Financial Policy Committee (FPC)

The FPC, within the Bank of England, is tasked with identifying, monitoring, and taking action to remove or reduce systemic risks to protect and enhance the resilience of the UK financial system. It works to support the Bank of England's objective of maintaining financial stability.

5. His Majesty's Treasury (HMT)

HMT has overall responsibility for the UK's financial system, including the institutional structure of financial regulation and the legislation that governs it, both domestically and internationally.

6. The Payment Systems Regulator (PSR)

Established in 2015, the PSR is the economic regulator for payment systems in the UK. It operates under the Financial Services (Banking Reform) Act 2013 and is a subsidiary of the FCA, but with its own statutory objectives:

- To promote competition in the markets for payment systems and services
- To promote innovation in payment systems
- To ensure payment systems are operated and developed in the interests of service users

The Regulated Activities Order (RAO)

The Financial Services and Markets Act 2000 (Regulated Activities) Order 2001, commonly known as the RAO, defines the activities and investments that fall under FCA regulation. The current regulated activities, as defined in Part II of the RAO, comprise:

1. Accepting deposits
2. Issuing electronic money
3. Effecting or carrying out contracts of insurance as principal
4. Dealing in investments (as principal or agent)
5. Arranging deals in investments

6. Arranging home finance activities
7. Operating a multilateral trading facility
8. Managing investments
9. Assisting in the administration and performance of a contract of insurance
10. Safeguarding and administering investments
11. Sending dematerialised instructions
12. Establishing collective investment schemes
13. Establishing stakeholder pension schemes
14. Providing basic advice on stakeholder products
15. Advising on investments
16. Advising on home finance activities
17. Lloyd's market activities
18. Entering funeral plan contracts
19. Entering into a home finance activity
20. Administering a home finance activity
21. Credit-related regulated activities
22. Operating an electronic system in relation to lending
23. Managing a UCITS
24. Acting as trustee or depositary of a UCITS
25. Managing an AIF
26. Acting as trustee or depositary of an AIF
27. Establishing, operating or winding up a personal pension scheme
28. Providing information about a person's financial standing

Specified investments, as defined in Part III of the RAO, include:

1. Deposits
2. Electronic money
3. Rights under a contract of insurance
4. Shares
5. Instruments creating or acknowledging indebtedness
6. Government and public securities
7. Instruments giving entitlement to investments
8. Certificates representing certain securities
9. Units in a collective investment scheme
10. Rights under a stakeholder pension scheme
11. Rights under a personal pension scheme
12. Options
13. Futures
14. Contracts for differences
15. Lloyd's syndicate capacity and syndicate membership
16. Rights under funeral plan contracts
17. Rights under regulated mortgage contracts
18. Rights under a home reversion plan
19. Rights under a home purchase plan
20. Rights to or interests in investments

Payment Services Regulations 2017

The Payment Services Regulations 2017 (PSRs 2017) came into force on 13 January 2018, implementing the revised Payment Services Directive (PSD2) in the UK. These regulations govern the authorisation and associated requirements for payment institutions and set the conduct of business rules for providing payment services.

The PSRs 2017 cover a wide range of payment services, including:

1. Services enabling cash to be placed on or withdrawn from a payment account
2. Execution of payment transactions
3. Issuing of payment instruments or acquiring of payment transactions
4. Money remittance
5. Account information services
6. Payment initiation services

Key aspects of the PSRs 2017 include:

- Defining payment services and specifying exclusions
- Establishing authorisation and registration requirements for payment service providers
- Setting standards for capital requirements and safeguarding of customer funds
- Outlining conduct of business requirements for payment services

- Granting the FCA and PSR powers for supervision and enforcement

The PSRs 2017 have introduced significant changes to the payments landscape, including:

- Open Banking: Requiring banks to share customer account data with authorised third-party providers, fostering innovation and competition in the payments sector.
- Strong Customer Authentication (SCA): Mandating additional security measures for certain electronic payments to reduce fraud.
- Expanded scope: Bringing new types of payment services, such as account information and payment initiation services, under regulation.

Payment Service Providers (PSPs) and Electronic Money Institutions (EMIs) - Differences

The main differences between payment service providers (PSPs) and electronic money institutions (EMIs) are:

1. Services offered:

- PSPs primarily focus on facilitating payment transactions, such as processing payments, money transfers, and merchant acquiring. They act as intermediaries in electronic transactions.

- EMIs are authorized to issue electronic money (e-money) in addition to providing payment services. E-money is electronically stored monetary value that can be used to make payments.

2. Licensing and regulation:

- PSPs are regulated under the Payment Services Regulations 2017 (PSRs 2017) in the UK.

- EMIs are regulated under both the PSRs 2017 and the Electronic Money Regulations 2011 (EMRs).

3. Capital requirements:

- EMIs typically have higher initial capital requirements (around €350,000) compared to PSPs.

- Capital requirements for PSPs vary based on the scope of services offered but are generally lower than for EMIs.

4. Holding customer funds:

- EMIs can hold customer funds in e-money accounts for extended periods.

- PSPs generally cannot hold customer funds long-term without an identifiable payment order.

5. Safeguarding requirements:

- Both have safeguarding requirements, but EMIs must safeguard funds for both e-money issuance and unrelated payment services separately.

6. Business models:

- EMIs can offer services like issuing prepaid cards and digital wallets linked to e-money accounts.

- PSPs focus more on facilitating transactions rather than storing value for customers.

7. Regulatory scope:

- EMIs are subject to additional regulations around e-money issuance and redemption.

- PSPs face regulations primarily focused on payment transaction processing and security.

Essentially, the key distinction is that EMIs can issue their own electronic money, while PSPs are limited to facilitating payment transactions without issuing e-money themselves. This leads to differences in licensing, capital requirements, and the types of services they can offer to customers.

The role of Account Information Service Providers

The role of account information service providers (AISPs) under the Payment Services Regulations 2017 (PSRs 2017):

Account information services (AIS) are defined as online services that provide consolidated information to a payment service user on one or more payment accounts held by that user with other payment service providers. The providers of these services are known as account information service providers (AISPs).

Key aspects of AISPs under PSRs 2017 include:

1. Regulatory status: AISPs are brought under regulation for the first time by PSRs 2017. This means they now need to be either registered or authorised by the Financial Conduct Authority (FCA).

2. Access to accounts: PSRs 2017 ensure that AISPs can receive access to payment accounts held by users with other payment service providers. This access is granted with the explicit consent of the account holder.

3. **Registration option**: Businesses that only provide account information services have the option to become registered account information service providers (RAISPs), which have fewer regulatory requirements than fully authorised firms.

4. **Consumer protection**: Regulating AISPs aims to improve consumer protection while promoting the development and use of innovative online payment services.

5. **Functionality**: AISPs can provide users with an electronic dashboard where they can view information from various payment accounts in a single place. They can also use account data to offer personalised comparison services and provide account information to third-party service providers like financial advisers or credit reference agencies, with the user's permission.

6. **Security requirements**: AISPs must adhere to strong customer authentication standards and secure communication methods as outlined in the regulatory technical standards.

7. **Professional indemnity insurance**: AISPs are required to hold professional indemnity insurance (PII).

The introduction of regulated AISPs under PSRs 2017 is intended to make it easier for consumers and businesses to manage their finances by allowing secure access to consolidated account information across multiple providers. This is part of the broader aim to increase innovation, improve market access for payment service providers, and enhance consumer protection in the financial services sector.

Based on the information provided, here are the key differences between Account Information Service Providers (AISPs) and Payment Initiation Service Providers (PISPs) in terms of their roles and responsibilities:

1. Services offered:

- AISPs provide online services that consolidate information from multiple payment accounts held by a user across different payment service providers. They offer a dashboard view of account information.

- PISPs initiate payments on behalf of users directly from their payment accounts. They provide an alternative method for online payments, competing with card payments.

2. Access to accounts:

- AISPs only access account information to provide consolidated views.

- PISPs can access accounts to initiate payment transactions.

3. Regulatory requirements:

- AISPs have the option to become registered account information service providers (RAISPs) with fewer regulatory requirements.

- PISPs must be fully authorised and meet higher capital requirements (minimum €50,000 initial capital).

4. Capital requirements:

- AISPs have no specific capital requirements if registered as RAISPs.

- PISPs must have a minimum of €50,000 in initial capital.

5. Scope of regulation:

- AISPs were brought under regulation to ensure they can receive access to payment accounts while maintaining security.

- PISPs were brought under regulation to ensure they receive access to accounts and to place security requirements on them.

6. User interaction:

- AISPs provide information services without moving funds.

- PISPs actively initiate payment transactions on behalf of users.

7. Authentication:

- Both require user consent, but PISPs specifically need user authentication to initiate payments.

8. Risk profile:

- PISPs generally have a higher risk profile due to their ability to initiate transactions, reflected in their stricter regulatory requirements.

Both AISPs and PISPs are required to hold professional indemnity insurance and comply with strong customer authentication standards and secure communication methods as outlined in regulatory technical standards.

In summary

The regulatory environment in the UK's financial services sector has evolved significantly over the past decades, moving from a system of self-regulation to a comprehensive framework overseen by multiple regulatory bodies. The creation of the FCA, PRA, and PSR, along with the implementation of the PSRs 2017, represents a concerted effort to enhance consumer protection, promote market integrity, and foster innovation in financial services.

As the industry continues to evolve, particularly with the rise of fintech and digital financial services, the regulatory landscape will undoubtedly continue to adapt. Financial firms must remain vigilant and proactive in their compliance efforts, ensuring they stay abreast of regulatory changes and maintain robust internal compliance functions.

The compliance department, once viewed as a necessary evil, has become an essential component of financial firms' operations. It serves not only as a safeguard against regulatory breaches but also as a valuable resource for navigating the complex and ever-changing regulatory environment. As such, understanding and effectively implementing regulatory requirements remains crucial for the success and sustainability of financial services firms in the UK.

Chapter 2 Anti-Money Laundering and Counter-Terrorist Financing

Anti-Money Laundering (AML) and Counter-Terrorist Financing (CTF) remain critical focus areas for financial services firms and regulators in the UK. As criminal tactics evolve and regulatory expectations increase, organisations must continuously enhance their AML/CTF frameworks to effectively mitigate risks.

Regulatory Landscape

The UK's AML/CTF regime is primarily governed by the Money Laundering, Terrorist Financing and Transfer of Funds (Information on the Payer) Regulations 2017 (MLRs), as amended. These regulations implement EU directives and international standards set by the Financial Action Task Force (FATF).

The Financial Conduct Authority (FCA) serves as the supervisory authority for financial services firms regarding AML/CTF compliance. As of 2022-23, approximately 18,000 firms were registered with the FCA for AML/CTF supervision.

HM Revenue & Customs (HMRC) supervises certain sectors including estate agencies, art market participants, and money service businesses not overseen by the FCA. HMRC supervised around 35,411 firms as of the 2022-23 reporting period.

Key Requirements

The MLRs mandate that regulated firms implement risk-based AML/CTF systems and controls. Core obligations include:

- Conducting customer due diligence (CDD)
- Ongoing monitoring of business relationships
- Reporting suspicious activity
- Staff screening and training
- Record keeping
- Internal controls and risk assessment

Customer Due Diligence

CDD forms the foundation of effective AML/CTF controls. Firms must verify customer identities and understand the nature of their business activities. The level of due diligence should be commensurate with the assessed money laundering and terrorist financing risks.

Standard CDD typically involves obtaining and verifying:

- Full name
- Date of birth
- Residential address
- Nature and purpose of the business relationship

For higher-risk situations, enhanced due diligence (EDD) measures are required. The MLRs specify certain scenarios necessitating EDD, including:

- Transactions with parties in high-risk third countries
- Politically exposed persons (PEPs)
- Complex or unusually large transactions
- Unusual patterns of transactions with no apparent economic purpose

EDD may entail additional steps such as:

- Obtaining further identification documents
- Verifying source of funds/wealth
- Enhanced ongoing monitoring
- Obtaining senior management approval to commence/continue the relationship

Risk Assessment

Firms must conduct and document both business-wide and customer risk assessments. Factors to consider include:

- Customer types
- Geographic areas of operation
- Products and services offered
- Delivery channels
- Transaction types

Risk assessments should be regularly reviewed and updated to reflect evolving threats and business changes.

Policies, Controls and Procedures

Robust written AML/CTF policies, controls and procedures are essential. These should cover:

- Risk assessment methodology
- Customer due diligence processes
- Transaction monitoring approach
- Internal and external suspicious activity reporting
- Record keeping standards
- Staff vetting and training programmes
- Compliance monitoring and audit

Senior management must approve AML/CTF policies and oversee their implementation.

Suspicious Activity Reporting

The MLRs require firms to appoint a nominated officer, often referred to as the Money Laundering Reporting Officer (MLRO). The MLRO is responsible for receiving internal suspicious activity reports and determining whether to file Suspicious Activity Reports (SARs) with the National Crime Agency (NCA).

Staff must promptly report any suspicions of money laundering or terrorist financing to the MLRO. The MLRO then evaluates whether the suspicion meets the reporting threshold. If so, a SAR must be submitted to the NCA via the online SAR portal.

Firms should have clear internal reporting procedures and provide regular training to staff on identifying and escalating suspicious activity.

Ongoing Monitoring

Effective ongoing monitoring is crucial for identifying unusual or potentially suspicious activity. This involves:

- Scrutinising transactions to ensure consistency with the firm's knowledge of the customer and their risk profile
- Keeping CDD information up to date
- Assessing the overall pattern of a customer's behaviour

Transaction monitoring systems should be calibrated based on the firm's risk assessment. Higher-risk customers and activities warrant enhanced scrutiny.

Record Keeping

Firms must maintain records of:

- Customer due diligence information
- Supporting evidence for transactions
- Internal and external suspicious activity reports

Records should be kept for at least five years from the end of the business relationship or occasional transaction. They must be readily retrievable to satisfy regulatory requests or law enforcement investigations.

Training

Staff training is a key component of AML/CTF compliance. Firms should provide regular, tailored training to ensure employees understand:

- Legal and regulatory obligations
- Money laundering and terrorist financing risks
- Internal AML/CTF policies and procedures
- How to identify and report suspicious activity

Training should be role-specific and updated to reflect new threats, typologies and regulatory developments.

Emerging Risks and Focus Areas

Cryptoassets

The MLRs were expanded in January 2020 to cover certain cryptoasset activities. Firms engaged in cryptoasset exchange services or custodian wallet provision must register with the FCA and comply with AML/CTF obligations.

Key requirements include:

- Conducting customer due diligence on cryptoasset transactions
- Monitoring for suspicious activity in cryptoasset transfers

- Implementing controls to mitigate risks associated with anonymity-enhanced cryptocurrencies

Sanctions Compliance

While distinct from AML/CTF, sanctions compliance is closely related. The UK's sanctions regime has evolved significantly following Brexit and in response to geopolitical events like the Russia-Ukraine conflict.

Firms must have robust systems to screen customers and transactions against applicable sanctions lists. This includes checking beneficial owners and conducting ongoing monitoring.

Environmental Crimes

There is growing recognition of the links between environmental crimes and money laundering. The illegal wildlife trade, illegal logging, and other environmental offences generate significant criminal proceeds.

Firms should consider environmental crime risks in their assessments and be alert to potential red flags in related sectors.

Regulatory Expectations and Enforcement

The FCA has repeatedly emphasised the importance of strong financial crime controls. Recent enforcement actions highlight several common failings:

- Inadequate customer due diligence and ongoing monitoring
- Failure to properly assess and mitigate risks

- Ineffective transaction monitoring systems
- Lack of adequate management information and oversight

In its 2022-23 anti-money laundering supervision report, HM Treasury noted that 18% of financial services firms assessed by the FCA were non-compliant with AML rules. Common issues included inadequate risk assessments, insufficient due diligence, and weak compliance monitoring.

The FCA has the power to impose substantial fines for AML/CTF failings. In 2022-23, it levied £197 million in AML-related fines across the financial services sector.

Future Developments

The UK government is consulting on updates to the MLRs and finalising a new effectiveness regime to better evaluate AML/CTF supervision. Key areas of focus include:

- Enhancing transparency around corporate structures and beneficial ownership
- Addressing risks associated with new technologies and business models
- Improving information sharing between the public and private sectors
- Strengthening the risk-based approach to supervision

Firms should monitor regulatory developments and be prepared to enhance their AML/CTF frameworks accordingly.

AML/CTF Summary

Effective AML/CTF compliance requires a holistic, risk-based approach. Firms must foster a strong compliance culture, implement robust controls, and continuously adapt to evolving threats and regulatory expectations. By doing so, they can play a crucial role in protecting the UK financial system from abuse by criminals and terrorists.

By maintaining robust systems and controls, staying informed about regulatory developments, and adopting a risk-based approach, firms can contribute to the integrity of the UK's financial system and play their part in the global fight against financial crime.

The FCA's ongoing work in this area, including its focus on effective supervision, technological innovation, and collaboration with other agencies, demonstrates the regulator's commitment to maintaining the UK's position as a leader in AML and CTF efforts.

Details of the relevant AML Regulations can be found in Appendix 1.

New FCA's Financial Crime Guide

Based on the updates to the FCA's Financial Crime Guide, here are some ways firms can prepare:

1. **Review proposed changes and assess impact**: Firms should carefully review the proposed updates, especially around sanctions, proliferation financing, transaction monitoring, cryptoassets and Consumer Duty. They should assess how these changes may impact their current financial crime systems and controls.

2. The **Proliferation Financing ("PF") changes**: Ensuring adequate coverage of PF considerations across the Guide, to highlight the MLR requirement to carry out PF risk assessments.

3. **Evaluate transaction monitoring arrangements**: Firms should assess if their current transaction monitoring systems are fit for purpose. Consider whether more sophisticated technologies like AI/machine learning could enhance detection of suspicious activity. Ensure data fed into automated systems is accurate and complete.

4. **Enhance sanctions compliance:**
   - Elevate senior management responsibility for sanctions risk management
   - Implement procedures to identify and escalate new sanctions risk events
   - Explore data analytics for detecting potential sanctions evasion
   - Ensure proper reporting of sanctions breaches to FCA and OFSI

5. **Update risk assessments:**
   - Ensure risk assessments are comprehensive, up-to-date and forward-looking
   - Include assessment of proliferation financing risks
   - Consider which business areas are most likely to interact with sanctioned individuals/entities

6. **Review cryptoasset-related controls**: For relevant firms, assess gaps in current controls around cryptoasset risks, especially for high-risk situations and blockchain analysis.

7. **Align with Consumer Duty**: Consider how financial crime controls align with new Consumer Duty obligations, e.g. enhancing customer fraud journeys.

8. **Enhance management information**: Ensure MI is sufficient for senior management to understand sanctions and other financial crime risks.

9. **Assess operational resilience**: Review systems dependencies and incident response plans related to financial crime controls.

10. **Plan for implementation**: Start planning how to implement necessary changes once the final updated Guide is published.

By taking these proactive steps, firms can better position themselves to meet the FCA's evolving expectations around financial crime compliance.

Consumer Duty Impacts

Based on the search results, there are several key implications of the new Consumer Duty obligations on financial crime systems and controls:

1. **Integration with existing frameworks**: Firms need to consider Consumer Duty obligations when reviewing their financial crime systems and controls. The FCA is proposing to incorporate references to Consumer Duty within the Financial Crime Guide.

2. **Focus on customer outcomes**: Firms must ensure their anti-financial crime programs deliver good customer outcomes and avoid causing foreseeable harm, in line with the Consumer Duty's cross-cutting rules.

3. **Enhanced customer communications**: Firms should review and monitor communications sent as part of anti-financial crime due diligence to ensure they meet Consumer Duty standards.

4. **Oversight of outsourced activities**: Even when anti-financial crime activities are outsourced, firms remain responsible for ensuring these meet Consumer Duty obligations.

5. Efficient sanctions implementation: Sanctions programs should be reviewed to ensure they can be implemented efficiently without unduly negatively impacting customers.

6. Improved customer journey: The FCA is proposing guidance around enhancing the customer fraud journey in line with Consumer Duty requirements.

7. Governance and oversight: Consumer Duty measures should be captured and monitored as part of firms' anti-financial crime program governance and oversight.

8. Balanced approach: Firms need to balance their financial crime prevention obligations with the need to provide positive outcomes for retail customers.

Note: Particular attention should be paid to key topics such as customer exits and treatment of Politically Exposed Persons (PEPs) in light of Consumer Duty obligations. See chapter 17.

10. Proportionate controls: Firms should ensure their financial crime controls are proportionate and consistent with their Consumer Duty obligations, avoiding overly rigid procedures that may negatively impact customers.

To prepare for these implications, firms should review their existing anti-financial crime frameworks, assess potential gaps, and implement necessary enhancements to ensure compliance with both financial crime regulations and Consumer Duty obligations.

Consumer Duty and the freezing of customer accounts

The Consumer Duty has several key implications for how firms handle the freezing of customer accounts due to suspected financial crime:

1. Proportionality and timeliness: The FCA expects firms to make account freezing less frequent, less protracted, and better communicated. This includes:

- Using better upfront onboarding and Know Your Customer controls to reduce unnecessary freezes.
- Conducting swifter and better-resourced investigations of suspicions
- Unfreezing accounts quickly when concerns are unfounded.

2. Communication: Firms should provide clearer communication to customers about account freezes, to the extent possible without "tipping off". This includes:

- Improving explanations given to customers about why their account is frozen.
- Providing better information on websites about how to report fraud and what actions to take.

3. Customer support: Firms need to provide appropriate support to customers affected by account freezes, including:

- Recognising the potential for customer distress and vulnerability.
- Avoiding unduly harsh judgments when customers complain.
- Considering how to support customers put into acute financial difficulties by the freeze.

4. Balancing obligations: Firms must balance their financial crime prevention duties with Consumer Duty obligations to deliver good customer outcomes. This may require:

- Reviewing sanctions screening tools and processes to ensure they don't unduly impact customers.
- Having reasonable service level agreements for reviewing sanctions alerts.

5. Oversight and monitoring: Consumer Duty measures should be incorporated into anti-financial crime program governance, including:

- Continually considering consumer outcomes in program management.
- Collecting and analysing data on customer impacts to identify unintended consequences.

6. Cultural shift: The Consumer Duty requires a change in mindset from a "check box" approach to financial crime prevention towards a more outcomes-focused approach that puts consumers at the heart of the business.

In summary, while firms still need to meet their financial crime obligations, the Consumer Duty requires them to do so in a way that is more considerate of customer impacts and outcomes, particularly around account freezing practices. This involves improving processes, communication, support, and oversight to minimise unnecessary customer harm while still effectively managing financial crime risks.

Chapter 3: The UK's Senior Managers and Certification Regime

The Senior Managers and Certification Regime

The Senior Managers and Certification Regime (SMCR) represents a significant shift in the UK's approach to financial services regulation. Introduced by the Financial Conduct Authority (FCA) and the Prudential Regulation Authority (PRA), this regime aims to enhance individual accountability within the financial sector, fostering a culture of responsibility and effective governance.

Origins and Implementation

The SMCR was initially applied to banks, building societies, credit unions, and PRA-designated investment firms in March 2016. Its scope was subsequently expanded to cover all FCA solo-regulated firms on 9 December 2019, replacing the previous Approved Persons Regime.

This expansion was a direct response to the recommendations made by the Parliamentary Commission on Banking Standards, which highlighted the need for clearer lines of responsibility and enhanced accountability in the wake of the 2008 financial crisis.

Key Components of the SMCR

The SMCR comprises three main elements:

1. The Senior Managers Regime
2. The Certification Regime
3. The Conduct Rules

The Senior Managers Regime

This component focuses on individuals who hold key roles within a firm. These roles, known as Senior Management Functions (SMFs), carry significant responsibilities for the firm's operations and conduct.

Senior Management Functions (SMFs)

SMFs are specific roles that require FCA approval before an individual can perform them. These functions vary depending on the firm's size and complexity but typically include roles such as:

- Chief Executive (SMF1)
- Executive Director (SMF3)
- Chair of the Risk Committee (SMF10)
- Compliance Oversight (SMF16)
- Money Laundering Reporting Officer (SMF17)

Statements of Responsibilities

Each Senior Manager must have a Statement of Responsibilities, which clearly outlines their role and the areas of the business for which they are accountable. This document serves as a single source of reference for the individual and the regulator.

Duty of Responsibility

Senior Managers have a statutory 'duty of responsibility'. This means that if a firm breaches an FCA requirement, the Senior Manager responsible for that area could be held personally accountable if they did not take reasonable steps to prevent or stop the breach.

The Certification Regime

This regime applies to employees whose roles have the potential to cause 'significant harm' to the firm or its customers. These roles are known as 'certification functions'.

Certification Process

Firms are responsible for identifying certification function roles and assessing the fitness and propriety of individuals in these roles at least annually. The firm must issue a certificate to each person deemed fit and proper, which is valid for up to 12 months.

Certification Functions

Examples of certification functions include:

- Significant Management Function
- Proprietary traders
- CASS oversight function
- Functions subject to qualification requirements
- Client dealing function
- Algorithmic trading

The Conduct Rules

The Conduct Rules set basic standards of good personal conduct, against which the FCA can hold people to account. These rules apply to all employees within a firm, except for ancillary staff.

First Tier – Individual Conduct Rules

1. You must act with integrity.
2. You must act with due skill, care and diligence.
3. You must be open and cooperative with the FCA, the PRA and other regulators.
4. You must pay due regard to the interests of customers and treat them fairly.
5. You must observe proper standards of market conduct.

Second Tier – Senior Manager Conduct Rules

SC1. You must take reasonable steps to ensure that the business of the firm for which you are responsible is controlled effectively.

SC2. You must take reasonable steps to ensure that the business of the firm for which you are responsible complies with the relevant requirements and standards of the regulatory system.

SC3. You must take reasonable steps to ensure that any delegation of your responsibilities is to an appropriate person and that you oversee the discharge of the delegated responsibility effectively.

SC4. You must disclose appropriately any information of which the FCA or PRA would reasonably expect notice.

Firm Classifications under SMCR

The FCA categorises firms into three types based on their size, complexity, and potential impact on consumers and markets:

1. Limited Scope Firms: These are subject to fewer requirements. Examples include sole traders and limited permission consumer credit firms.

2. Core Firms: This category applies to most firms regulated by the FCA.

3. **Enhanced Firms:** These are the largest and most complex firms, subject to additional SMCR requirements.

Practical Implementation of SMCR

Identifying and Appointing Senior Managers

Firms must identify which of their senior staff are performing SMFs and ensure they are approved by the FCA. This process involves:

1. Determining which SMFs apply to the firm
2. Identifying who will perform these functions
3. Preparing and submitting applications to the FCA
4. Creating Statements of Responsibilities for each Senior Manager

Certification Process

For the Certification Regime, firms need to:

1. Identify certification function roles
2. Conduct fit and proper assessments
3. Issue certificates to staff deemed fit and proper
4. Renew these certificates annually

Training and Communication

Firms must ensure that all relevant staff are aware of and understand the Conduct Rules. This typically involves:

1. Providing training on the Conduct Rules
2. Implementing processes to identify and report Conduct Rule breaches
3. Ensuring Senior Managers understand their enhanced responsibilities

Regulatory Reporting and Record-Keeping

Firms have ongoing obligations under the SMCR, including:

- Submitting Form D to notify the FCA of any changes to a Senior Manager's responsibilities or details
- Reporting any disciplinary action taken against individuals for Conduct Rule breaches
- Maintaining records of fitness and propriety assessments for certified staff

Impact on Firm Culture and Governance

The SMCR aims to drive cultural change within firms by:

- Encouraging a sense of personal responsibility among senior staff
- Promoting clearer organisational structures and lines of accountability
- Fostering a culture of openness and effective challenge
- Enhancing the overall standard of conduct within the financial services industry

Challenges and Considerations

While the SMCR has been largely successful in its aims, firms have faced some challenges in implementation:

- Ensuring all relevant staff are identified and included in the regime
- Maintaining up-to-date and accurate Statements of Responsibilities

- Balancing individual accountability with collective decision-making
- Adapting governance structures to align with SMCR requirements

Future Developments

The FCA continues to refine and develop the SMCR. Recent and potential future developments include:

- Extending the regime to appointed representatives
- Enhancing requirements around non-financial misconduct
- Increasing focus on diversity and inclusion within senior management
- Adapting the regime to address emerging risks and technologies in the financial sector

The Main Challenges

The main challenges firms face in complying with the Senior Managers and Certification Regime (SMCR) include:

1. Time and resource demands: SMCR affects a large proportion of staff and compliance requires significant time and resources, especially for tasks like preparing Statements of Responsibilities for senior managers.

2. Increased costs: Firms need to invest in training, consultants, legal advice, and technology solutions to implement SMCR effectively.

3. **Potential impact on productivity**: The personal accountability aspect may make some managers more hesitant in decision-making, which could slow down business activities.

4. **Implementation challenges**: Poor implementation can lead to uncertainty among managers about their responsibilities and liabilities.

5. **Governance structure and culture changes**: Shifting from collective to individual responsibility models can be difficult, especially for partnerships used to shared accountability.

6. **Documentation requirements**: Creating and maintaining clear Statements of Responsibilities, job descriptions, and ensuring consistency across documents is time-consuming.

7. **Fitness and Propriety assessments**: Developing rigorous processes for initial and annual F&P assessments, including obtaining regulatory references and criminal record checks.

8. **Delays in the Senior Manager approval process**: Although improvements have been made, firms have raised concerns about delays in getting regulatory approval for Senior Manager appointments.

9. **Ensuring clarity of responsibilities**: Firms must clearly allocate and document responsibilities among Senior Managers, including mandatory prescribed responsibilities.

10. Ongoing compliance: Maintaining up-to-date documentation, conducting annual certifications, and keeping the FCA directory current require continuous effort.

To address these challenges, many firms are turning to automation and technology solutions to streamline processes and reduce administrative burdens. The regulators are also reviewing the regime to identify potential improvements while preserving its core aims.

How has the SMCR Changed?

Based on the search results and my knowledge, the Senior Managers and Certification Regime (SMCR) has evolved in several ways since its initial implementation:

1. Expanded scope: The SMCR was first introduced in 2016 for banks, building societies, credit unions and PRA-designated investment firms. It was then extended to insurers in 2018, and finally to all FCA solo-regulated firms in December 2019, bringing an additional 47,000 firms under the regime.

2. Evaluations and reviews: Both the FCA and PRA have conducted evaluations of the SMCR since its implementation:

- In 2019, the FCA conducted interviews with 60 senior managers and certified staff at banks.
- In 2020, the PRA gathered evidence from 120 deposit-taking institutions and insurers.

These reviews generally found that the SMCR was having a positive effect on individual behaviour and accountability.

3. Cultural impact: The regime has had a significant impact on firm culture, particularly in smaller and medium-sized firms. It has led to more formal operational processes, such as key decisions being taken in minuted meetings to evidence processes to the regulator.

4. HR practices: The SMCR has influenced HR practices, including changes to employment contracts, recruitment processes, and the full employee lifecycle from hiring to exit.

5. Ongoing refinement: Regulators have continued to refine and develop the SMCR. For example, the PRA announced changes to the Handbook for PRA Approved Persons after taking over their role.

6. New conduct rules: Additional conduct rules have been introduced over time. For instance, a new SMCR conduct rule related to the Consumer Duty is set to be introduced in July 2023.

7. Regulatory approach: The SMCR has become an integral part of the regulators' approaches to supervising and regulating financial services firms.

8. International influence: The UK's implementation of the SMCR has influenced other countries to introduce or develop similar accountability regimes.

9. Ongoing review: In 2023, a comprehensive review of the SMCR was launched by the FCA and PRA, in conjunction with HM Treasury, to assess its effectiveness and consider potential improvements.

Overall, while the core principles of the SMCR have remained consistent, the regime has evolved through expansion, refinement, and integration into regulatory and business practices across the financial services industry.

Summary

The Senior Managers and Certification Regime represents a significant shift in the UK's approach to financial regulation. By focusing on individual accountability and promoting a culture of responsibility, the SMCR aims to enhance trust in financial services and protect consumers and markets. As the regime continues to evolve, firms must remain vigilant in their compliance efforts and embrace the cultural changes it seeks to instil.

Chapter 4: Authorisation and Regulatory Framework

Authorisation and Regulatory Framework

In the United Kingdom, the financial services industry operates under a comprehensive regulatory framework designed to protect consumers, maintain market integrity, and ensure financial stability. At the heart of this framework is the authorisation process, which is essential for firms and individuals wishing to conduct regulated activities.

The General Prohibition

The cornerstone of the UK's financial regulatory system is the general prohibition, which makes it an offence to carry out regulated activities without proper authorisation. This principle is enshrined in the Financial Services and Markets Act 2000 (FSMA) and applies to all individuals and firms operating within the UK financial services sector.

Pathways to Authorisation

There are several routes through which an entity can gain authorisation to conduct regulated activities in the UK:

1. **Part IV Permission**: Obtaining permission under Part IV of FSMA to carry out regulated activities.

2. **EEA Passport Rights**: Exercising passporting rights under relevant EU directives, although this has been significantly impacted by Brexit. No longer available.
3. **Treaty Rights**: Exercising rights under international treaties, which may have also been affected by the UK's exit from the European Union.

Categories of Regulated Persons

The regulatory framework encompasses various categories of individuals and entities:

- Individuals employed by regulated firms
- Self-employed individuals ('one-man bands')
- Regulated firms
- Recognised professional bodies (e.g., accountants, solicitors)
- Collective investment schemes
- Clearing houses and exchanges

Dual Regulation: FCA and PRA

The UK financial services sector is overseen by two primary regulators: the Financial Conduct Authority (FCA) and the Prudential Regulation Authority (PRA). Some firms are subject to dual regulation, requiring authorisation from both bodies.

For dual-regulated firms, a single application process is in place to streamline the procedure:

- Paper applications for dual-regulated firms should be submitted to the PRA.
- Paper applications for FCA-only regulated firms go directly to the FCA.
- Online applications through the regulators' Online Notifications and Applications (ONA) system are automatically routed to the appropriate regulator(s).

Principles-Based Regulation

The UK has gradually shifted towards a more principles-based approach to regulation. This approach emphasises high-level principles rather than prescriptive rules, allowing for greater flexibility and encouraging firms to focus on outcomes rather than mere compliance with specific regulations.

The 11 Principles for Businesses

The FCA has established 11 core principles that all regulated firms must adhere to:

1. Integrity
2. Skill, care, and diligence
3. Management and control
4. Financial prudence
5. Market conduct
6. Customers' interests
7. Communications with clients
8. Conflicts of interest

9. Customers: relationships of trust
10. Clients' assets
11. Relations with regulators

These principles serve as the foundation for ethical and responsible business practices in the financial services sector.

The "Consumer Duty", introduced mid-2023, embedded a further Principle; Principle 12 states that "a firm must act to deliver good outcomes for retail customers".

Statements of Principle for Approved Persons

In addition to the principles for businesses, there are seven Statements of Principle that apply to approved persons. The Appointed Representative regime still uses the APER designations.

1. Integrity
2. Skill, care, and diligence
3. Observance of proper standards of market conduct
4. Dealings with regulators
5. Effective control (for significant influence functions)
6. Due skill in managing the business (for significant influence functions)
7. Compliance with regulatory standards (for significant influence functions)

Payment Services Firms

The regulation of payment services firms has become increasingly important with the rise of financial technology (FinTech) and digital payment solutions. In the UK, payment services are regulated under the Payment Services Regulations 2017, which implement the EU's Second Payment Services Directive (PSD2).

Types of Payment Services Firms

There are several categories of payment services firms:

1. Authorised Payment Institutions (APIs): Firms authorised to provide a wide range of payment services.
2. Small Payment Institutions (SPIs): Smaller firms with limited transaction volumes that are subject to a lighter regulatory regime.
3. Registered Account Information Service Providers (RAISPs): Firms that provide account information services without handling customer funds.
4. Electronic Money Institutions (EMIs): Firms that issue electronic money and may also provide payment services.

Authorisation Process for Payment Services Firms

To become authorised, payment services firms must:

1. Submit a detailed application to the FCA, including business plans, governance arrangements, and risk management procedures.
2. Demonstrate compliance with capital requirements, which vary depending on the type of firm and services offered.
3. Establish robust safeguarding measures to protect customer funds.
4. Implement strong customer authentication procedures and secure communication protocols.

Variation of Permissions (VoP)

A Variation of Permission (VoP) is a process through which an authorised firm can change the scope of its regulated activities. This may involve adding new activities, removing existing ones, or altering the conditions under which the firm operates.

Reasons for Seeking a VoP

Firms might seek a VoP for various reasons:

- Expanding into new areas of business
- Responding to changes in market conditions or regulatory requirements
- Restructuring the business or altering its focus
- Ceasing certain activities that are no longer part of the firm's strategy

The VoP Process

The VOP Process is very similar to the normal authorisation application and should not be overlooked.

1. Assessment: The firm evaluates its current permissions and determines the changes required.

2. Application: A formal application is submitted to the FCA (or PRA for dual-regulated firms) detailing the proposed changes and rationale.

3. Business Plan: The firm provides an updated business plan reflecting the impact of the proposed changes.

4. Regulatory Business Plan: A comprehensive document outlining how the firm will comply with regulatory requirements under the new permissions.

5. Review: The regulator assesses the application, often requesting additional information or clarifications.

6. Decision: The regulator decides to grant, partially grant, or refuse the VoP application.

7. Implementation: If approved, the firm implements the necessary changes to systems, controls, and procedures to accommodate the new permissions.

Considerations for VoP Applications

When applying for a VoP, firms should consider:

- The impact on capital requirements and financial resources
- Changes to governance structures and senior management responsibilities
- Additional compliance and reporting obligations
- The need for new or updated policies and procedures
- Potential effects on existing customers and business relationships

How did the PSRs affect FCA Authorisation?

The Payment Services Regulations 2017 (PSRs 2017) introduced several key changes to the authorisation process for payment service providers in the UK:

1. New categories requiring authorisation:

- The PSRs 2017 created new categories of regulated payment services, including account information services (AIS) and payment initiation services (PIS). Firms providing these services now require authorisation or registration with the FCA.

2. Authorisation requirements:

- Payment institutions providing payment services as a regular occupation or business activity must be either Authorised as an Authorised Payment Institution (API) or registered as a Small Payment Institution (SPI), depending on their transaction volumes.

  - APIs need full FCA authorisation if they expect to process over €3 million in payments annually.

  - SPIs can register with lighter requirements if they expect less than €3 million in annual payment volumes.

3. Application process:

- Firms must submit detailed information to the FCA as part of the authorisation/registration process, including:
- Business plans and forecasts
- Governance arrangements and internal controls
- Safeguarding measures for customer funds
- IT systems and security policies
- Anti-money laundering procedures

4. Ongoing compliance:

- Authorised/registered firms must comply with conduct of business rules, capital requirements, safeguarding rules, and other ongoing obligations under the PSRs 2017.

5. Re-authorisation:

- Existing payment institutions had to apply for re-authorisation under the new PSRs 2017 regime by April 2018.

6. Passporting changes:

- The PSRs 2017 initially maintained EU passporting rights, allowing UK Authorised firms to operate in other EEA countries. However, this changed after Brexit.

7. Transitional provisions:

- The regulations included transitional provisions to allow existing providers time to become compliant with the new authorisation requirements.

8. Exclusions:

- Certain activities are excluded from regulation, but firms relying on exclusions may need to notify the FCA in some cases.

9. FCA powers:

- The FCA was given enhanced supervisory and enforcement powers over payment service providers.

In summary, the PSRs 2017 expanded the scope of regulated payment activities, introduced more stringent authorisation processes, and imposed new ongoing compliance obligations on payment service providers in the UK. This aimed to enhance consumer protection and align the UK regime with EU standards under PSD2.

Changes to the Conduct of Business Rules

The Payment Services Regulations 2017 (PSRs 2017) made several key changes to the conduct of business rules for payment service providers in the UK compared to the previous 2009 regulations. Some of the main changes included:

1. Expanded scope of regulated payment services:

- Added two new regulated payment services: payment initiation services and account information services.
- This brought providers of these services under regulation for the first time.

2. Enhanced information requirements:

- More detailed requirements on the information that must be provided to customers before and after payment transactions.
- New requirements to provide information on charges and exchange rates used.

3. Stronger customer authentication:

- Introduced requirements for "strong customer authentication" for electronic payments, with more stringent security procedures.

4. Liability changes:

- Reduced customer liability for unauthorized transactions from £50 to £35 in most cases.
- New liability provisions for payment initiation service providers.

5. Complaints handling:

- Reduced the time limit for resolving complaints from 8 weeks to 15 business days in most cases.
- Required payment service providers to inform customers about alternative dispute resolution options.

6. Access to payment accounts:

- New rules requiring banks to provide payment initiation and account information service providers with access to customer payment account data (with customer consent).

7. Operational and security risk management:

- More detailed requirements for firms to assess operational and security risks and implement appropriate mitigation measures.

8. Incident reporting:

- New obligations to report major operational or security incidents to the regulator.

9. Open banking provisions:

- Laid the groundwork for open banking by requiring account providers to allow third-party access to account data and payment initiation (with customer consent).

10. Safeguarding requirements:

- Enhanced rules on safeguarding customer funds, including new options for how funds can be protected.

These changes aimed to enhance consumer protection, promote innovation and competition in payments, and align UK rules with the EU's revised Payment Services Directive (PSD2). The conduct rules apply to all payment service providers, including banks, e-money institutions and payment institutions.

In summary

The authorisation and regulatory framework in the UK financial services sector is designed to maintain high standards of conduct, protect consumers, and ensure the stability of the financial system. As the industry evolves, particularly with the growth of FinTech and digital financial services, the regulatory landscape continues to adapt. Firms must stay informed of these changes and maintain robust compliance programmes to navigate the complex regulatory environment successfully.

Chapter 5: The Role of Compliance

The Role of Compliance

In the ever-evolving landscape of financial services, compliance has emerged as a critical function, yet it remains a relatively young profession. When asked about their occupation, compliance professionals often find themselves explaining their role to the uninitiated. While those working within compliance departments of larger firms may feel they have a comprehensive understanding of their specific remit, truly exceptional compliance professionals must possess a broad knowledge base spanning numerous areas.

The world of compliance is rife with buzzwords that can confuse both support staff and those in front, middle, or back-office roles. Terms such as 'compliance function', 'compliance department', 'culture of compliance', 'compliance manager', and 'compliance officer' are frequently used, but their meanings can vary between organisations. In most firms, there is no definitive list of responsibilities for a compliance manager or officer, leading to generalised or vague job descriptions.

Defining Compliance

To comprehend the world of compliance, we must first establish a clear understanding of what compliance entails and its role within an organisation. By distilling the terminology used in various legislation and guidance, we can formulate our own robust definition.

A standard dictionary definition of compliance typically refers to adherence to rules or regulations. In industries where safety is paramount, compliance often means conforming to internal policies or operational standards to eliminate potential hazards.

The Basel Committee on Banking Supervision provided a definition of compliance risk in 2005:

"The risk of legal or regulatory sanctions, material financial loss, or loss of reputation a bank may suffer as a result of its failure to comply with laws, regulations, rules, related self-regulatory organisation standards, and codes of conduct applicable to its banking activities (together, compliance laws, rules and standards)".

While this definition is high-level and specific to the banking sector, we can refine it for everyday use:

"Compliance within our firm is the function of identifying relevant legislative, regulatory, and best practice requirements, and then implementing the necessary changes to our systems and controls to facilitate ongoing adherence to these obligations."

Responsibility for Compliance

Unlike other departments such as IT, finance, or administration, the question of who is responsible for compliance within a firm has multiple answers. It is not simply the compliance officer's responsibility, as compliance is a far-reaching discipline. Like risk management, the responsibility for achieving compliance rests with the entire staff.

One could argue that a compliance department should not exist in any firm, as compliance, being the responsibility of all staff, could be relegated to internal audit in larger firms or the executive function in smaller firms. The Financial Conduct Authority's (FCA) principles of good regulation state: "A firm's senior management is responsible for ensuring that its business complies with regulatory requirements".

The FCA's Enforcement Guide (EG) further emphasises this point: "The FCA is committed to ensuring that senior managers of firms fulfil their responsibilities. The FCA expects senior management to take responsibility for ensuring firms identify risks, develop appropriate systems and controls to manage those risks, and ensure that the systems and controls are effective in practice".

Interestingly, if one were to scour the FCA Handbook, they would find no explicit statement that the compliance officer or compliance department is "responsible" for compliance. In fact, official regulatory references to a "compliance officer" are scarce. This demonstrates the unique nature of the compliance industry within financial services – a profession that has grown to be massively resourced across financial institutions nationwide, despite having an ill-defined role.

While this semantic point may spark lengthy discussions among compliance staff in larger financial institutions, for most firms, the compliance officer is typically a member of senior management, directors, or owners, and therefore shares ultimate responsibility with their peers and regulators.

The Compliance Manager's Role

Managing a compliance department can be likened to dancing among moving blades. Compliance managers must provide advice and guidance to senior management while ensuring the firm operates efficiently and smoothly. They must also prevent senior management from bypassing them and making ill-informed regulatory decisions in their absence.

It is crucial to establish early on that while the compliance manager or officer may be accountable and may or may not consult other staff members regarding the effective implementation of rules and regulations, ultimately, everyone within the firm is responsible for compliance.

In some firms, the relationship with the regulator is jointly managed with the firm's general counsel or legal representative. However, in most firms, the Compliance Manager's responsibilities extend beyond day-to-day compliance activities. These responsibilities include:

- Owning the relationship with regulators
- Developing the compliance and regulatory framework within the firm

- Providing regulatory guidance and advice to firm members
- Ensuring the compliance culture is embedded throughout the firm's infrastructure
- Assessing and monitoring the compliance department's activities for adequacy and appropriateness

Key Responsibilities of a Compliance Manager

The role of Compliance Manager or officer carries a significant burden of responsibility, including:

1. Developing a thorough understanding of the firm and the entirety of its regulatory impact
2. Determining best practice standards from across the industry and aligning them with regulatory and legislative requirements to create a compliant sales model
3. Identifying how to apply requirements and practice standards without restricting growth or innovation while operating within the regulatory framework
4. Clearly documenting compliance maintenance methods and monitoring, assessing, and appreciating measures through manuals, policies, procedures, work plans, scripts, newsletters, bulletins, and internet attachments
5. Effectively delivering training and awareness activities to ensure all staff understand their compliance obligations and are up to date with the latest developments

6. Staying informed of regulatory developments and changes that impact the firm currently and, in the future, and making necessary framework adjustments
7. Implementing remedial action where instances of non-compliance or other problems are identified
8. Conducting file reviews, training and competence assessments, and monitoring sales activity to ensure a consistent, compliant, and fair approach
9. Engaging in regulatory reporting to meet specific requirements, such as the Retail Mediation Activities Return (RMAR) or changes through the Online Notification and Application (ONA) system for personnel authorisations
10. Measuring, assessing, and identifying compliance risks to evaluate the impact and likelihood of particular risks materialising, including understanding the risks, consequences, adequate controls, and mitigation plans
11. Providing adequate, robust, and coherent management information to senior management to enable them to execute their management responsibilities compliantly and correctly
12. Becoming a confidante, friend, adviser, and consultant on all regulatory matters

Characteristics of an Effective Compliance Manager

An effective Compliance Manager should possess a range of attributes and skills:

1. **Confidence**: The ability to challenge the status quo and stand firm against intimidation or pressure to bend rules.

2. **Training delivery**: The capacity to convey compliance messages clearly and positively, explaining the rationale and necessity for everyone's involvement.

3. **Communication**: The skill to interact effectively with people at all levels within the organisation, fostering respect and understanding.

4. **Regulatory knowledge**: A comprehensive understanding of the various regulators affecting the firm, providing a clear grasp of the origins and reasons behind rules.

5. **Attention to detail**: The ability to interpret new rules, conduct monitoring analyses and investigations, and provide creative solutions rather than simply saying "no".

6. **Gravitas**: Credibility when making decisions, backed by experience and a consistent approach to explanations.

7. **IT and report writing skills**: Competence in using IT systems efficiently for report writing, data analysis, and preparation of management information.

8. **Decision-making**: The ability to quickly understand new situations and make informed decisions or confidently defer decision-making when necessary.

9. **Diplomacy**: The art of negotiation and persuasion, avoiding threats, intimidation, or bullying tactics.

10. **Patience**: A key attribute in dealing with various challenges and personalities.

11. **Enthusiasm**: A genuine passion for the role, which helps in managing the associated challenges and complaints.

Working as a compliance manager, officer, or consultant can be rewarding, much like vocations in teaching or nursing. While compliance itself may not be rocket science, years of questionable sales practices and sensationalist leadership in sales psychology have created numerous issues in their delivery. These "techniques" and "sales management methods" may not individually cause significant harm, but collectively, they can mislead or confuse potential clients, potentially leading them to act against their best interests.

In conclusion, the role of compliance and the Compliance Manager is multifaceted and crucial in today's financial services landscape. It requires a unique blend of skills, knowledge, and personal attributes to navigate the complex regulatory environment while supporting the business objectives of the firm. As the industry continues to evolve, so too will the role of compliance, making it an ever challenging and dynamic field for those who choose to pursue it.

Benefits of Using 'Compliance Consultant' Regulatory Consultancy
In the complex and ever-evolving landscape of UK financial services regulation, engaging ***Compliance Consultant*** regulatory consultancy can provide numerous advantages for firms across various sectors.' Compliance Consultant' offer specialised expertise and impartial guidance, helping businesses navigate the intricate web of regulatory requirements and best practices.

Expertise and Specialisation

'Compliance Consultant' possess in-depth knowledge of the UK's financial services regulatory framework.
They employ experts who are well-versed in the latest regulations, including those set forth by the Financial Conduct Authority (FCA) and the Prudential Regulation Authority (PRA). This specialised expertise ensures that firms receive accurate and up-to-date advice tailored to their specific needs.

Impartial Guidance

Unlike in-house compliance teams, '*Compliance Consultant*' offer an objective perspective on regulatory matters.

This impartiality is crucial for identifying potential blind spots and providing unbiased recommendations for improvement. Firms can benefit from fresh insights and innovative solutions that may not be apparent from an internal viewpoint.

Cost-Effectiveness

Engaging '*Compliance Consultant*' can be more cost-effective than maintaining a full-time in-house compliance team, especially for smaller firms or those with fluctuating regulatory needs. Consultancies offer flexible services that can be scaled up or down as required, allowing firms to manage their regulatory compliance costs more efficiently.

Risk Mitigation

'*Compliance Consultant*' help firms identify and mitigate potential risks before they become significant issues. By conducting thorough assessments and implementing robust compliance frameworks, these consultancies assist in reducing the likelihood of regulatory breaches and the associated financial and reputational damages.

Streamlined Compliance Processes

'Compliance Consultant' can help firms streamline their compliance processes, improving efficiency and reducing the burden on internal resources. They often bring best practices and innovative technologies to enhance regulatory reporting, monitoring, and documentation.

Regulatory Liaison

'Compliance Consultant' have established relationships with regulatory bodies and can act as intermediaries between firms and regulators. This can be particularly valuable during regulatory investigations, applications for authorisation, or when seeking clarification on complex regulatory matters.

Ongoing Support and Training

'Compliance Consultant' offer ongoing support and training programmes to help firms stay abreast of regulatory changes and maintain compliance. This continuous learning approach ensures that firms are well-prepared to adapt to new regulatory requirements and industry best practices.

By leveraging the expertise and services of *'Compliance Consultant'*, firms can enhance their compliance posture, mitigate risks, and focus on their core business activities with greater confidence in their regulatory standing.

Common Compliance Challenges

Based on the search results and my analysis, some of the most common compliance challenges faced by financial institutions in the UK include:

1. Anti-Money Laundering (AML) and Financial Crime Controls:

- Inadequate business-wide and individual customer risk assessments
- Poor customer due diligence (CDD) practices, including failure to update CDD throughout customer relationships
- Insufficient enhanced due diligence (EDD) for high-risk customers
- Inadequate transaction monitoring and suspicious activity reporting

2. Operational Resilience:

- Ensuring critical business services can continue during disruptive events
- Identifying and managing risks from third-party dependencies
- Meeting new regulatory requirements around operational resilience reporting

3. Data Protection and Privacy:

- Complying with GDPR and other data protection regulations
- Ensuring proper data security measures are in place
- Managing data across complex IT systems

4. Conduct and Culture:

- Embedding a culture of compliance throughout the organisation
- Ensuring fair treatment of customers and good customer outcomes
- Managing conduct risk, especially in areas like sales practices

5. Regulatory Change Management:

- Keeping up with the pace of regulatory changes, including post-Brexit divergence
- Implementing new rules and requirements in a timely manner
- Updating policies, procedures and controls to reflect regulatory changes

6. Technology and Cybersecurity:

- Managing risks from new technologies like AI and cloud computing
- Ensuring robust cybersecurity defences and incident response capabilities
- Complying with technology-related regulations

7. Environmental, Social and Governance (ESG):

- Meeting new ESG disclosure and reporting requirements
- Integrating ESG considerations into risk management frameworks
- Avoiding greenwashing allegations

8. Resource Constraints:

- Allocating sufficient budget and resources to compliance functions
- Recruiting and retaining skilled compliance professionals
- Balancing compliance needs with other business priorities

9. Off-Channel Communications:

- Monitoring and recording communications across new channels
- Preventing use of unauthorized communication methods

10. Sanctions Compliance:

- Keeping up with rapidly changing sanctions regimes
- Implementing effective sanctions screening and monitoring

Financial institutions need to take a holistic, risk-based approach to addressing these challenges, leveraging technology and data analytics where possible. Maintaining strong governance, fostering a culture of compliance, and ensuring proper training for staff are also critical success factors.

Essential Skills

The essential skills and qualifications for a compliance manager in the UK:

Qualifications:

1. A bachelor's degree, typically in subjects like accounting, economics, law, business management, or a related field. Some employers may prefer candidates with advanced degrees like an MBA or law degree.

2. Professional certifications such as:
   - Certified Anti-Money Laundering Specialist (CAMS)
   - Certified Compliance Manager (CCM)
   - Certified Regulatory Compliance Manager (CRCM)
   - Certifications from the International Compliance Association (ICA)
   - Investment Compliance Diploma (CISI)

3. Strong understanding of relevant laws, regulations and industry standards

Essential Skills:

1. **Regulatory knowledge and expertise** - Ability to stay up to date with regulatory changes and understand their implications

2. **Communication skills** - Ability to effectively communicate complex regulatory information to all levels of the organisation

3. **Attention to detail** - For examining laws/regulations and checking compliance

4. **Problem-solving and analytical skills** - To assess risks and develop compliance solutions

5. **Ethical awareness and integrity** - To uphold high standards of conduct

6. **Relationship building** - To work effectively with other departments and external regulators

7. **Leadership and influence** - To drive the compliance agenda across the organisation

8. **IT and reporting skills** - For data analysis and preparing management information

9. **Project management** - To handle multiple compliance initiatives

10. **Decision-making** - Ability to make sound judgments on compliance matters

Other Important Attributes:

- Confidence to challenge non-compliance at all levels
- Diplomacy and negotiation skills
- Patience and enthusiasm for the role
- Ability to see the bigger picture of how compliance fits into business objectives

Continuous learning and staying updated on regulatory changes is also crucial for success in this role. Many compliance managers gain experience through related roles in risk, audit or legal departments before moving into senior compliance positions.

In closing, a robust compliance function is not merely a regulatory requirement but a foundational element of sound business practice. It ensures that firms remain aligned with evolving regulatory landscapes while maintaining their integrity and reputation in the financial industry. It is always worthwhile grounding the department practices into the evolving and developing regulatory landscape and this is done by independent assessment and reporting.

Compliance Consultant can be contacted via email: info@complianceconsultant.org

Chapter 6: The Benefits of Compliance

The Benefits of Compliance

In the ever-evolving landscape of financial services, regulatory compliance has become an indispensable aspect of business operations. Far from being a mere bureaucratic hurdle, effective compliance offers a multitude of benefits that extend beyond mere adherence to rules. This chapter explores the manifold advantages of robust compliance practices, elucidating why they are crucial for both clients and companies in the financial sector.

Client Benefits

At its core, regulatory compliance is designed to ensure that customers receive fair treatment and are fully informed about the risks, benefits, and challenges associated with their financial decisions. This client-centric approach yields several key advantages:

Enhanced Transparency: Improved systems, including customer-focused reporting rules, agreements, and notifications, make the services provided more transparent and credible to clients. This transparency fosters trust and helps clients make more informed decisions about their financial affairs.

Fairness and Integrity: By maintaining a firm's integrity and treating clients fairly, companies not only increase customer loyalty but also encourage referrals of other high-quality clients. This approach can provide a sustainable competitive advantage in the long term.

Risk Awareness: Compliance regulations ensure that clients are made aware of all potential risks associated with their investments or financial products. This knowledge empowers clients to make decisions that align with their risk tolerance and financial goals.

Protection from Malpractice: Stringent compliance measures safeguard clients from potential malpractice or misconduct by financial service providers. This protection is crucial in maintaining the integrity of the financial system and protecting vulnerable consumers.

Company Benefits

While many regulatory requirements focus on improving the customer experience, numerous compliance measures are aimed at enhancing a firm's internal systems and controls. These improvements can lead to significant benefits for the company:

Improved Governance: A well-managed firm with effective and proportionate governance systems in place can better identify accountability at all levels and ensure proper oversight of controls. This structure facilitates a successful risk and compliance model feedback loop, leading to more informed decision-making.

Cost Efficiency: Robust compliance and efficient internal arrangements reduce the likelihood of fines and the need for additional resources to administer procedures and processes. This efficiency can lead to lower operational costs and improved profitability.

Reputational Enhancement: In an era where reputation is increasingly important in the financial services world, strong compliance practices can mitigate negative press and enhance a firm's standing in the industry. The Financial Conduct Authority (FCA) has indicated its intention to measure and assess firms' reputations, making this aspect even more critical.

Regulatory Capital Benefits: Strong and demonstrable systems and controls often allow for greater leniency under regulatory capital regimes. This can free up capital for other business initiatives or investments.

Crisis Management: Compliance involvement in business continuity planning and crisis management can ensure minimal negative impact and maximum positive emphasis on any reputational issues that may arise.

The Hidden Value of Compliance

The true value of compliance often lies in its ability to prevent crises and mitigate risks before they materialise. This preventative function, while less visible, is crucial for the long-term success and stability of financial firms.

Audit Trail and Justification: Maintaining a log of all compliance-related advice, queries, and recommendations provides an audit trail and justifies the effectiveness of the compliance department. This documentation can be invaluable during regulatory inspections or internal audits.

Knowledge Dissemination: By circulating highlights and extracts from regulatory consultation papers with easy-to-follow narratives, compliance managers can increase awareness of regulated activities throughout the firm. This proactive approach to education can foster a culture of compliance across all levels of the organisation.

Complaint Handling: Operating a clear, straightforward, and effective complaints department helps protect the firm from potentially vindictive or irresponsible clients. It also provides valuable management information that can be used to improve products and services.

The Cost-Benefit Analysis of Compliance

While the benefits of compliance are numerous, it's important to acknowledge that implementing and maintaining robust compliance systems does come with costs. These can include:

- Staff costs (salaries, bonuses, pensions, benefits)
- Office space and equipment
- IT systems and software
- Training and development expenses

- Indirect costs (e.g., time spent on compliance activities rather than revenue-generating tasks)

However, when weighed against the potential costs of non-compliance – including fines, legal fees, reputational damage, and loss of business – the investment in compliance often proves to be highly cost-effective.

The Evolving Role of Compliance Managers

The perception of compliance managers has evolved significantly in recent years. Far from being seen as mere enforcers of rules, modern compliance professionals play a crucial role in shaping business strategy and managing risk.

Strategic Advisors: Compliance managers are increasingly involved in business planning and product development, ensuring that new initiatives are compliant from inception.

Ethical Champions: Many compliance professionals see their role as an ethical challenge, helping to steer their organisations towards practices that are not just legally compliant but also ethically sound.

Risk Management Experts: The integration of Governance, Risk, and Compliance (GRC) has elevated the role of compliance managers in overall risk management strategies.

Problem Solvers: Compliance work often requires creative thinking to implement regulatory requirements in a way that works within the firm's operational framework.

Impact on Reputation Risk

Effective compliance can have a significant positive impact on a company's reputation in several critical ways:

1. **Builds trust and credibility:** Adhering to regulations and ethical standards demonstrates a commitment to integrity and responsible business practices. This fosters trust among customers, investors, employees and other stakeholders.

2. **Enhances brand image**: Compliance with quality, safety and ethical standards can differentiate a company positively from competitors and attract consumers who prioritise responsible corporate conduct.

3. **Boosts investor confidence:** Investors prefer companies that operate within legal bounds, as it reduces risks of legal liabilities and regulatory fines. Strong compliance signals stability and good governance.

4. **Mitigates reputational damage**: A robust compliance program can help prevent scandals, violations or crises that could severely damage a company's reputation if they occurred.

5. **Improves relationships with regulators**: Regulators tend to view companies with strong compliance track records more favourably, potentially leading to less stringent oversight.

6. **Demonstrates corporate responsibility**: Compliance with environmental, labour and other regulations showcases a company's commitment to being a good corporate citizen.

7. **Attracts and retains talent**: Employees prefer to work for companies known for ethical practices and regulatory adherence.

8. **Provides competitive advantage**: Strong compliance can be a differentiator, especially in highly regulated industries or when working with risk-averse partners/clients.

9. **Supports long-term viability**: By reducing legal/regulatory risks and building stakeholder trust, effective compliance contributes to a company's sustainability and success over time.

10. **Enables focus on core business**: A systematic compliance approach allows leadership to focus more on innovation and growth rather than constantly managing crises.

In today's environment of increased scrutiny and activism, maintaining a strong compliance program is crucial for protecting and enhancing corporate reputation. It demonstrates a company's commitment to operating ethically and responsibly, which is increasingly important to stakeholders across the board.

Investor Confidence

Effective compliance has a significant positive impact on investor confidence in several ways:

1. **Builds trust and credibility**: Adhering to regulations and ethical standards demonstrates a company's commitment to integrity and responsible business practices. This fosters trust among investors, who prefer companies that operate within legal bounds.

2. **Enhances transparency:** Compliance improves systems and reporting, making services more transparent and credible to investors. This transparency allows investors to make more informed decisions.

3. **Mitigates risks**: A robust compliance program helps identify, assess and mitigate risks inherent in financial operations. This risk reduction is attractive to investors, as it safeguards their investments.

4. **Improves governance**: Well-managed firms with effective compliance systems can better identify accountability and ensure proper oversight. This improved governance structure is appealing to investors.

5. **Protects reputation**: Strong compliance practices can mitigate negative press and enhance a firm's standing in the industry. A good reputation is crucial for attracting and retaining investors.

6. **Demonstrates ethical behaviour**: Compliance shows a company's dedication to being a good corporate citizen. Many investors prefer to associate with companies known for ethical practices.

7. **Reduces likelihood of fines/penalties**: Effective compliance reduces the chances of regulatory fines or legal issues, which can negatively impact investor returns.

8. **Enhances long-term viability**: By reducing legal/regulatory risks and building stakeholder trust, compliance contributes to a company's sustainability and success over time.

9. **Provides competitive advantage**: Strong compliance can differentiate a company from competitors, especially in highly regulated industries.

10. **Aligns with investor values**: Many investors prioritise companies with strong ethical standards and compliance track records.

11. **Supports fair treatment of investors**: Compliance rules often aim to ensure fair treatment of investors, which naturally increases their confidence in the company.

In essence, a strong culture of compliance serves as a foundation for building and maintaining investor trust. It signals to investors that the company takes its responsibilities seriously and is committed to operating in an ethical, transparent, and accountable manner.

Examples of Compliance Failures and their consequences

Certainly. Here are some notable examples of compliance failures and their consequences:

1. ABN Amro - €480 million fine (2021)

- Failure: Inadequate anti-money laundering (AML) controls
- Consequence: Dutch prosecutors fined ABN Amro €480 million for failing to identify accounts involved in money laundering and not reporting suspicious transactions.

2. NatWest - £264.7 million fine (2021)

- Failure: Money laundering regulation breaches

- Consequence: The Financial Conduct Authority (FCA) fined NatWest for failing to properly monitor the activity of a commercial customer who deposited £365 million, including £264 million in cash.

3. Credit Suisse - £147.2 million fine (2021)

- Failure: Due diligence deficiencies related to loans for the Republic of Mozambique
- Consequence: The FCA fined Credit Suisse for financial crime due diligence failings linked to $1.3 billion in loans tainted by corruption.

4. JPMorgan - $125 million fine (2021)

- Failure: Failure to maintain and preserve written communications
- Consequence: The Securities and Exchange Commission (SEC) fined JPMorgan for widespread failures in preserving employee communications about securities business matters on personal devices.

5. Deutsche Bank - $120 million fine (2021)

- Failure: Violations of the Foreign Corrupt Practices Act
- Consequence: Deutsche Bank paid $120 million to settle charges of engaging foreign officials and their associates as third-party intermediaries to obtain and retain global business.

6. Santander UK - £107.7 million fine (2022)

- Failure: Serious and persistent gaps in anti-money laundering controls
- Consequence: The FCA fined Santander for ineffective systems to verify customer information and monitor account activity, affecting over 560,000 business customers.

9. TSB - £10.9 million fine (2024)

The TSB case is a prime example of the severe consequences that can result from compliance failures:

1. **Financial penalty**: TSB was fined £10.9 million by the Financial Conduct Authority (FCA) for failing to treat customers in arrears fairly.

2. **Compensation costs**: The bank had to pay £99.9 million in redress to 232,849 affected customers across various products including mortgages, overdrafts, credit cards, and loans.

3. **Reputational damage**: The FCA described TSB's systems and controls as "woeful", potentially harming the bank's reputation.

4. **Regulatory scrutiny**: The failings were uncovered during an independent review ordered by the FCA, leading to increased regulatory oversight.

5. **Operational costs**: TSB had to implement a comprehensive programme to resolve these issues, costing £105 million.

6. Extended impact: The issues persisted from June 2014 to March 2020, demonstrating how compliance failures can have long-lasting effects.

7. Missed opportunities: Despite becoming aware of potential problems in December 2016, TSB failed to take effective action until 2020, highlighting the importance of prompt response to compliance issues.

This case underscores the multifaceted impact of compliance failures, affecting not just finances but also reputation, customer trust, and regulatory relationships. It serves as a stark reminder of the importance of robust compliance systems and the potential costs of neglecting them.

These examples demonstrate that compliance failures can result in severe financial penalties, reputational damage, and increased regulatory scrutiny. They highlight the importance of maintaining robust compliance systems and controls, particularly in areas such as anti-money laundering, due diligence, and record-keeping.

Compliance in Risk Management

Compliance plays a crucial role in risk management for organisations. Here are some ways compliance and risk management are interconnected:

1. **Identifying and mitigating regulatory risks**: Compliance helps identify legal and regulatory requirements that apply to an organisation. This allows companies to proactively address potential regulatory risks before they materialise into violations or penalties.

2. **Establishing internal controls**: Compliance programs typically involve implementing policies, procedures and controls to ensure adherence to laws and regulations. These same controls often help mitigate operational and financial risks as well.

3. **Promoting a culture of ethics and risk awareness**: Effective compliance programs foster an organisational culture that values ethical behaviour and risk management. This makes employees more likely to identify and report potential risks.

4. **Providing a framework for risk assessment**: Compliance requirements often necessitate regular risk assessments. These assessments help identify both compliance risks and other business risks.

5. **Enhancing governance:** Compliance programs strengthen overall corporate governance by ensuring oversight, accountability and transparency. This supports broader risk management efforts.

6. **Protecting reputation**: By preventing regulatory violations and unethical conduct, compliance helps protect an organisation's reputation - a key risk management priority for many companies.

7. **Supporting decision-making**: Compliance insights inform risk-based decision making by highlighting potential legal/regulatory implications of business activities.

8. **Enabling early detection**: Compliance monitoring and auditing can uncover risk issues early, allowing for timely mitigation.

9. **Providing assurance**: Compliance reports and certifications provide assurance to leadership, boards and external stakeholders about the organisation's risk management.

10. **Integrating with enterprise risk management**: Many organisations are integrating compliance and risk management functions to take a more holistic view of organisational risks.

In essence, while compliance focuses specifically on adherence to laws and regulations, it serves as a key component of an organisation's overall risk management strategy. An effective compliance program helps identify, assess and mitigate a wide range of risks beyond just regulatory compliance.

Summary

The benefits of compliance extend far beyond mere regulatory adherence. Effective compliance practices enhance client trust, improve operational efficiency, protect reputational assets, and contribute to the long-term sustainability of financial firms. While the costs of compliance can be significant, they pale in comparison to the potential consequences of non-compliance.

As the financial services landscape continues to evolve, compliance will remain a critical function, helping firms navigate complex regulatory environments while fostering trust and integrity in the financial system. By embracing compliance as a strategic asset rather than a necessary burden, firms can position themselves for success in an increasingly regulated and scrutinised industry.

Chapter 7: The Compliance Contract

The Compliance Contract

In the realm of financial services, establishing a clear and comprehensive compliance framework is paramount. This chapter delves into the crucial elements of what we might term "The Compliance Contract" - the foundational agreements and documents that define the role, responsibilities, and expectations of the compliance function within an organisation.

The Compliance Mission Statement

At the heart of any effective compliance programme lies a well-crafted mission statement. This concise document serves as a beacon, guiding the compliance department's efforts and communicating its purpose to the wider organisation.

A robust compliance mission statement should:

1. Clearly articulate the fundamental aims of the compliance department
2. Be tailored for both internal and external audiences
3. Outline priority tasks and methodologies for team members
4. Express how the department will support the business without compromising integrity

5. Minimise subjective statements to avoid misinterpretation

When drafting your mission statement, consider the following example:

"Our compliance department is committed to safeguarding the integrity of our organisation by ensuring adherence to regulatory requirements, fostering a culture of ethical behaviour, and supporting sustainable business growth through effective risk management."

Compliance Mission Statement

The key elements to include in a compliance mission statement are:

1. A succinct definition of the fundamental aims of the compliance department.

2. Separate versions for internal and external audiences:
   - Internal version: Describes priority tasks and focus methodology for team members
   - External version: Expresses how the department will support the business without compromising integrity

3. Clear articulation of the department's purpose and goals.

4. A brief explanation of how the department will support the rest of the business.

5. Minimal use of subjective statements to avoid misinterpretation.

6. A focus on the department's commitment to regulatory compliance and ethical behaviour.

7. An emphasis on the department's role in supporting sustainable business growth.

8. A statement on fostering a culture of compliance within the organisation.

9. A mention of the department's approach to risk management.

10. A concise overview of the department's key responsibilities.

The mission statement should be concise, clear, and avoid jargon or overly technical language. It should serve as a guiding principle for the compliance department and communicate its value to the wider organisation.

The Compliance Charter

Building upon the mission statement, the compliance charter serves as a more comprehensive document that outlines the department's role, responsibilities, and relationship with the rest of the organisation. This charter acts as both a promotional tool and a high-level service agreement between the compliance department and other business units.

Key Components of a Compliance Charter

1. Definition of Compliance Risk: Clearly explain what constitutes compliance risk within your organisation. For example: "Compliance risk is the potential for legal or regulatory sanctions, material financial loss, or reputational damage resulting from failure to comply with applicable laws, regulations, and standards."

2. Scope and Limitations: Outline the specific areas of responsibility for the compliance department, such as:

- Regulatory oversight
- Financial crime prevention
- Conduct risk management
- Financial promotions review
- Complaints handling

3. Compliance Department Objectives: Highlight the high-level goals of the department, which may include:

- Maintaining an effective regulatory framework
- Upholding ethical standards
- Developing and implementing policies and procedures
- Conducting monitoring and gathering management information
- Fostering proactive dialogue with staff across the organisation

4. Authority and Powers: Clearly state the compliance department's authority, including:

- Oversight capabilities
- Access to documents and records

- Right to expect cooperation from other departments

5. Interactions with Regulators: Outline how the compliance department will manage relationships with regulatory bodies, such as the Financial Conduct Authority (FCA) and the Prudential Regulation Authority (PRA).

6. Compliance Responsibilities for the Organisation: Detail the expectations for all staff members regarding compliance, including:

- Reporting potential rule breaches
- Escalating suspicions of financial crime
- Seeking guidance on regulatory matters

7. Performance Measurement: Establish key performance indicators (KPIs) to assess the effectiveness of the compliance function.

8. Reporting and Escalation Procedures: Define how compliance issues will be reported and escalated within the organisation.

9. Charter Approval and Review Process: Outline the process for approving and periodically reviewing the charter.

Implementing the Compliance Contract

Once you have developed your mission statement and charter, it's crucial to ensure they are effectively communicated and integrated into the organisation's culture.

Senior Management Buy-In

Securing the support of the board and senior management is essential. Present the compliance contract as a strategic asset that will help protect the organisation and support sustainable growth. Highlight how a robust compliance framework can:

1. Mitigate regulatory risks
2. Enhance the firm's reputation
3. Improve operational efficiency
4. Support informed decision-making

Communication and Training

Develop a comprehensive communication plan to ensure all staff members are aware of the compliance department's role and responsibilities. This may include:

1. Induction training for new employees
2. Regular compliance updates via email or intranet
3. Targeted training sessions for high-risk areas or departments
4. Annual compliance refresher courses

Consider creating a series of compliance e-bulletins that highlight:

- Recent regulatory developments
- Top compliance challenges and how to address them
- Common mistakes in areas such as financial promotions
- Frequently asked compliance questions

Measuring Effectiveness

To demonstrate the value of the compliance function and identify areas for improvement, establish a set of metrics to measure the effectiveness of your compliance programme. These might include:

1. Number of regulatory breaches identified and remediated
2. Timeliness of regulatory reporting
3. Staff completion rates for compliance training
4. Results of internal compliance audits
5. Feedback from business units on compliance support

Evolving the Compliance Contract

As the regulatory landscape and your organisation change, it's important to regularly review and update your compliance contract. Consider conducting an annual review of your mission statement and charter, involving key stakeholders from across the business.

During this review, assess:

1. Changes in regulatory requirements or expectations
2. Shifts in the organisation's risk profile or business model
3. Feedback from staff and management on the compliance function
4. Emerging best practices in compliance management

By maintaining a dynamic and relevant compliance contract, you can ensure that your compliance function remains an effective and valued partner in your organisation's success.

Communicate the importance of compliance

To effectively communicate the importance of compliance to senior management, consider the following approaches:

1. Present compliance as a strategic asset:

- Highlight how a robust compliance framework can mitigate regulatory risks and protect the organisation from potential sanctions or reputational damage.
- Emphasise that effective compliance supports sustainable business growth and can enhance the firm's reputation in the market.

2. Secure senior management buy-in:

- Explain how compliance can improve operational efficiency and support informed decision-making.
- Demonstrate how a strong compliance culture can be a competitive advantage in the financial services industry.

3. Use clear, non-technical language:

- Avoid jargon and "regulator speak" when presenting to senior management.
- Use the "house language" that resonates with your organisation's culture and values.

4. Develop a comprehensive compliance charter:

- Create a document that outlines the compliance department's role, responsibilities, and value to the organisation.

- Ensure the charter is endorsed by senior management to give it credibility across the firm.

5. Establish performance metrics:

- Develop key performance indicators (KPIs) that demonstrate the effectiveness of the compliance function.
- Regularly report on these metrics to show the tangible benefits of compliance efforts.

6. Highlight regulatory developments:

- Keep senior management informed about changes in the regulatory landscape that could impact the business.
- Provide insights on how compliance can help navigate these changes effectively.

7. Showcase success stories:

- Share examples of how effective compliance has prevented issues or improved business processes.
- Demonstrate the return on investment in compliance resources and initiatives.

8. Conduct targeted training:

- Offer tailored compliance training sessions for senior management to help them understand their specific responsibilities.
- Use real-world scenarios and case studies to illustrate the importance of compliance.

9. Leverage internal allies:

- Collaborate with other departments like Legal, Risk Management, and Internal Audit to present a unified message on the importance of compliance.

10. Proactively address concerns:

- Anticipate and address potential objections or concerns that senior management may have about compliance initiatives.
- Present compliance as a solution to business challenges rather than a hindrance to operations.

By implementing these strategies, you can effectively communicate the value of compliance and gain the necessary support from senior management to build a strong compliance culture within your organisation.

Summary

The compliance contract, comprising a well-crafted mission statement and comprehensive charter, forms the foundation of an effective compliance programme. By clearly defining the role, responsibilities, and expectations of the compliance function, organisations can foster a culture of compliance that supports sustainable growth and protects against regulatory risks.

Remember, the key to success lies not just in creating these documents, but in effectively communicating them, securing buy-in from all levels of the organisation, and continuously evolving them to meet the changing needs of your business and the regulatory environment.

Chapter 8: Mapping Your Compliance Landscape

Mapping Your Compliance Landscape

In the realm of financial services compliance, understanding your regulatory landscape is paramount. Gone are the days when Compliance Managers could operate in isolation, poring over rulebooks in dimly lit offices. Today's effective compliance professional must have a comprehensive grasp of how their firm fits into the broader regulatory context.

To provide exemplary compliance services, one must first map out the compliance landscape. This process, while extensive and at times complex, is crucial for establishing a robust foundation for your compliance department. It ensures that all policies, controls, processes, and procedures are built on solid ground.

Charting Your Territory

To begin this mapping exercise, procure a fresh notebook and divide it into the following key sections:

Group Structure

Detail each entity within your group, including:

- Appointed representatives
- Introducer appointed representatives

- Subsidiary companies
- Joint venture partners

Internal Organisation

List out:

- Each business unit within each entity
- Support departments across the organisation

External Partnerships

Identify all external service providers, including outsourced functions such as:

- IT services
- Paraplanning
- Legal counsel
- Banking services

Regulatory Jurisdiction

Outline the regulatory landscape in which you operate. For most UK firms, this will primarily be the United Kingdom, potentially extending to Europe. However, many firms now offer offshore investment services, so it's crucial to consider all relevant jurisdictions.

Within each jurisdiction, identify:

- All relevant regulators (e.g., Financial Conduct Authority, Prudential Regulation Authority)
- Standards-setting bodies and quasi-regulatory organisations (e.g., The Pensions Regulator, Financial Ombudsman Service)

- Applicable legislation, regulations, and codes of practice

Products and Services

Catalogue the full range of products and services offered across your organisation, including:

- Front office activities (e.g., client-facing roles, sales)
- Middle office functions (e.g., risk management, compliance)
- Back office operations (e.g., settlement, accounting)
- Specific offerings such as general insurance, mortgages, financial planning, and investment management

Regulatory Documentation

List common documentation used across all entities for regulatory matters, such as:

- Disclosure documents
- Financial promotions
- Client agreements
- Terms of business

This exercise will quickly reveal that the role of a Compliance Manager extends far beyond traditional compliance boundaries. It encompasses aspects of legal, marketing, governance, company secretarial, and office management functions. While it's beneficial to engage with these additional areas, it's wise to approach them diplomatically rather than assertively.

The Value of Comprehensive Understanding

As you delve into gathering this information and immersing yourself in the knowledge of various departments, colleagues may question why you need to understand aspects like IT systems, capital treatment, or HR processes.

It's crucial to confidently explain that a broad understanding of the firm's operations helps contextualise compliance activities and aids in identifying compliance risks and potential breaches.

While a deep understanding of financial promotions regulations is essential, it's equally important to comprehend the content of those promotions and the products or services they advertise. Merely applying rules without understanding context is insufficient in today's complex financial landscape.

Moreover, by showing genuine interest in other departments' operations, you'll gain credibility among colleagues. However, it's vital to approach this process with an open mind, avoiding premature criticism of existing processes before fully understanding their purpose and function.

Navigating Challenges

During your fact-finding mission, you may encounter difficulties obtaining certain information. This typically stems from two scenarios:

1. The information is irrelevant to your business and can be disregarded.
2. The information is relevant but not readily available, indicating a potential gap that requires further investigation.

It's crucial to maintain a neutral stance during this initial data-gathering phase. Avoid forming opinions, criticising processes, or proposing solutions prematurely. Your primary goal at this stage is to map out the bigger picture, not to address individual issues that may arise.

The Regulatory Landscape

While a one-size-fits-all rulebook for financial services would simplify matters, the diversity of the industry in the UK and Europe makes this impractical. However, we can outline a general framework to capture essential information:

Regulators and Industry Bodies

In the UK, the primary financial services regulators are the Financial Conduct Authority (FCA) and the Prudential Regulation Authority (PRA). However, depending on your firm's activities, you may also need to consider:

- The Pensions Regulator (TPR)
- Information Commissioner's Office (ICO)
- Financial Ombudsman Service (FOS)
- Financial Services Compensation Scheme (FSCS)

Legislative Environment

Key legislation to consider includes:

- Financial Services and Markets Act 2000 (FSMA)
- Money Laundering Regulations 2017
- Data Protection Act 2018
- Bribery Act 2010
- Senior Managers and Certification Regime (SMCR)

Financial Products and Services

The range of products and services offered by UK financial firms is vast, potentially including:

- Investments (e.g., stocks, bonds, funds)
- Insurance (life, general, health)
- Mortgages and equity release
- Pensions and retirement planning
- Banking services
- Foreign exchange and money transfer

Each of these areas comes with its own regulatory considerations and requirements.

Measuring Effectiveness

Here are some ways financial institutions can ensure their compliance mapping is effective:

1. **Conduct comprehensive risk assessments:**
   Perform firm-wide risk assessments to identify and evaluate potential compliance risks associated with the institution's activities, customers, products, and geographies. This helps prioritise compliance efforts effectively.

2. **Maintain an up-to-date regulatory inventory:**
   Create and regularly update a comprehensive inventory of all applicable laws, rules, regulations and obligations that apply to the institution across all relevant jurisdictions. This "rule register" or "obligations register" forms the foundation for compliance mapping.

3. **Implement robust regulatory change management:**
   Establish processes to constantly monitor for regulatory changes, assess their applicability and impact on existing obligations, and update compliance frameworks accordingly. Consider using RegTech solutions to automate aspects of this process.

4. **Map obligations to internal controls and policies:**
   Systematically link regulatory obligations to the institution's internal controls, policies and procedures to ensure proper implementation. This helps identify any gaps in compliance coverage.

5. **Integrate compliance with broader risk management:** Ensure compliance risk management is integrated with the overall operational risk management framework for a holistic view of risks. Consider organisational structures that facilitate this integration.

6. **Leverage technology and data analytics:** Utilise compliance technology solutions and data analytics to automate manual processes, improve accuracy of compliance assessments, and gain predictive insights into emerging risks.

7. **Develop horizontal expertise:** Move beyond siloed business unit-based compliance to develop horizontal expertise in key compliance areas like AML, consumer protection, etc..

8. **Maintain clear roles and responsibilities:** Clearly define compliance roles and responsibilities across the three lines of defence model to avoid gaps or overlaps.

9. **Implement robust KYC/KYB processes:** Have strong customer due diligence procedures and regularly rescreen customers against sanctions lists and other relevant databases.

10. **Conduct regular testing and monitoring:**

    Perform ongoing compliance monitoring and testing to verify the effectiveness of controls and identify any issues.

11. **Foster a culture of compliance:**

    Ensure strong tone from the top and active board oversight to embed compliance into the organisational culture.

12. **Maintain audit trails:**

    Document compliance activities, decisions and rationales to demonstrate regulatory adherence.

By implementing these best practices, financial institutions can develop a comprehensive, risk-based approach to compliance mapping that is responsive to regulatory changes and integrated with broader risk management efforts. Regular reviews and leveraging of technology are key to maintaining effectiveness over time.

Common Challenges

Here are some common challenges financial institutions face when mapping their compliance landscapes:

1. **Regulatory complexity and constant change:**

   The regulatory environment is increasingly complex and constantly evolving. Keeping track of new regulations, updates to existing ones, and enforcement trends across multiple jurisdictions can be overwhelming. This makes it challenging to maintain an up-to-date and comprehensive compliance map.

2. **Lack of visibility across departments:**

   Regulatory risk management often involves multiple departments, including legal, compliance, IT, finance, and operations.

   Ensuring these departments work together effectively and share information can be a complex organisational challenge. Without clear visibility, different departments might implement and enforce compliance policies inconsistently.

3. **Resource constraints:**

   Allocating adequate resources, including budget and personnel, for compliance activities can be challenging, especially for smaller institutions. This can limit the ability to conduct thorough compliance mapping and keep it updated.

4. **Siloed approaches:**

   Many organisations still have siloed approaches to compliance, with different business units managing their own regulatory obligations. This can lead to duplication of efforts, inconsistencies, and gaps in compliance coverage.

5. **Technology integration:**

   While technology can greatly aid compliance mapping, integrating new compliance systems with existing IT infrastructure can be complex and time-consuming. Legacy systems may not be compatible with modern compliance management tools.

6. **Data management:**

   Gathering, organising, and analysing the vast amount of data required for comprehensive compliance mapping can be overwhelming. Ensuring data quality and consistency across different systems and departments is often a significant challenge.

7. **Assessing and prioritising risks:**

   Effectively assessing the likelihood and severity of compliance risks, and then prioritizing them based on their potential impact, requires sophisticated risk assessment tools and methodologies. Many organisations struggle with this aspect of compliance mapping.

8. **Keeping pace with business changes:**

   As businesses evolve, enter new markets, or introduce new products and services, the compliance landscape changes. Ensuring that compliance mapping keeps pace with these business changes can be challenging.

9. **Cross-border complexities:**

   For institutions operating across multiple jurisdictions, mapping compliance obligations becomes even more complex due to varying regulatory requirements and cultural differences.

10. **Demonstrating effectiveness:**

    Proving the effectiveness of compliance mapping efforts to regulators and stakeholders can be challenging, especially in the absence of standardised metrics or benchmarks.

To address these challenges, financial institutions should consider adopting a risk-based approach to compliance, leveraging advanced technologies like GRC platforms and AI, fostering cross-departmental collaboration, and maintaining a proactive stance towards regulatory changes. Regular reviews and updates of the compliance map, along with ongoing training and awareness programs, are also crucial for effective compliance landscape mapping.

In summary

Mapping your compliance landscape is a fundamental step in establishing an effective compliance function. It provides a comprehensive overview of your firm's regulatory obligations and helps identify potential risk areas. By understanding the broader context in which your firm operates, you'll be better equipped to navigate the complex world of financial services compliance and provide valuable insights to your organisation.

Remember, this mapping exercise is not a one-time task but an ongoing process. As your firm evolves and the regulatory landscape shifts, regular reviews and updates to your compliance map will be necessary to ensure continued effectiveness and relevance.

Chapter 9: Rules Mapping

Rules Mapping: A Comprehensive Guide for Compliance Managers

In the complex world of financial services, understanding and navigating the regulatory landscape is paramount. Rules mapping is a crucial process that helps compliance managers identify, organise, and manage the various regulatory requirements applicable to their firm. This chapter will explore the intricacies of rules mapping, providing a comprehensive guide for compliance professionals in the UK financial services sector.

Identifying the Regulatory Landscape

The first step for a compliance manager is to identify the regulatory territory in which their firm operates. This involves understanding the structure of the organisation and its relationships with various entities. While this chapter primarily focuses on UK authorised and regulated firms, the principles can be applied to other jurisdictions with appropriate modifications.

Key Areas to Consider:

1. UK branch offices
2. Overseas branches or representative offices
3. Other UK regulated firms within the group
4. Non-UK regulated firms within the group
5. Special purpose vehicles
6. Investment funds, including distributor-influenced funds
7. Joint ventures

8. Appointed representative firms
9. Dormant firms with existing liabilities

It's crucial to maintain a comprehensive log of all relevant details, even if immediate responsibilities are not apparent. This information can prove invaluable in case of rapid changes or unexpected situations.

Understanding Distributor-Influenced Funds

Distributor-influenced funds are a unique category that merits special attention. These funds are typically created for clients of a particular distributor, often an adviser firm. They may be bespoke or based on existing funds tailored for the distributor. While fund administration and management are outsourced, the distributor may retain some influence over the fund's operation.

Key Characteristics:

- Ability to influence the hiring or removal of the delegated investment manager
- Participation in investment committees
- Power to appoint or remove the Authorised Corporate Director (ACD)

These funds can take various structures, including Open-Ended Investment Companies (OEICs) and insurance funds.

Essential Data Requirements

To effectively perform their role, compliance managers should gather and maintain the following information for each relevant entity:

1. **Full Company Name**: Including correct corporate designation and explanations of abbreviations
2. **Previous Names**: Important for understanding historical context and client references
3. **Registered Address**: Required for official documents and agreements
4. **Place of Business Address(es):** Necessary for monitoring visits and understanding the firm's physical presence
5. **Key Contact Information**: Including website and email domains
6. **Corporate Data**: Incorporation details, tax registration numbers, and business registration numbers
7. **Regulatory Information**: Details of local regulators, approval dates, and regulatory capital requirements
8. **Financial Year End**: Important for reporting deadlines
9. Ownership and Control: Information on significant influencers and controllers
10. **Stock Market Listing**: If applicable, and associated rules
11. **Subsidiaries, Representative Offices, and Branches**: Understanding the firm's structure and regulatory obligations
12. **Powers of Attorney**: Identifying who has legal authority to act on behalf of the entity

13. **Senior Management**: Details of those requiring regulatory approval
14. **Committees and Official Bodies**: Understanding internal governance structures
15. **Compliance Officer and Money Laundering Reporting Officer (MLRO)**: Key contacts for regulatory matters
16. **Internal and External Auditors**: Important for coordinating compliance efforts
17. **Legal Advisers and Corporate Service Providers**: Understanding key partnerships and outsourcing arrangements

Understanding Business Units

For larger organisations with multiple business units, additional information may be required:

- Management compliance concerns
- Specific products, services, or activities
- Main income-generating activities
- Unique selling points
- Documentation used at point of sale or post-sale
- Target client base or segment
- Advertising and marketing methods
- IT systems
- Most valued clients
- Top deals of the previous 12 months
- Complaints and challenges
- Governance policies and procedures

- Conflicts of interest and regulatory issues
- Major changes (past and planned)

Risk Management and Mitigation

When developing risk management programmes, consider the following elements:

1. Specific responsibilities for each legislative requirement
2. Impact assessment of legislation on the firm
3. Identification of key risks
4. Controls in place for each risk
5. Weaknesses in the control framework
6. Action plans to address identified weaknesses
7. Review frequency for reassessment
8. Overall risk rating for each legislative area

Constructing Rules Matrices

There are two primary approaches to constructing rules matrices:

1. Bottom-Up Approach: Starting at the activity level and considering all applicable legislative and regulatory impacts.

2. Top-Down Approach: A more detailed exercise, searching for applicability of specific laws to the business.

The choice of approach depends on the size and complexity of the organisation. Larger companies with diverse operations may benefit from the top-down approach, while smaller firms with a single main line of business might find the bottom-up approach more suitable.

Sample Rules Map

A typical rules map can be created using a spreadsheet format. Column headings can reference the Financial Conduct Authority (FCA) handbooks, such as:

1. SYSC (Senior Management Arrangements, Systems and Controls)
2. COBS (Conduct of Business Sourcebook)
3. BIPRU (Prudential Sourcebook for Banks, Building Societies and Investment Firms)
4. INSPRU (Prudential Sourcebook for Insurers)

Rows can represent different functions or areas of activity within the firm, such as:

- Trading desks
- Middle office
- Settlement
- Life sales
- Pensions sales
- Investment sales
- Mortgages

This matrix allows for easy identification of which handbooks apply to specific areas of the business. For firms with international operations, similar matrices can be created for each jurisdiction.

The rules mapping process for compliance managers in UK financial services firms include:

1. Identifying the regulatory landscape:

- Understand the structure of the organisation and its relationships with various entities
- Identify all relevant entities including UK branches, overseas offices, regulated firms within the group, special purpose vehicles, investment funds, joint ventures, etc.

2. Gathering essential data for each relevant entity:

- Full company name, previous names, registered address, place of business
- Corporate data, regulatory information, ownership details
- Key contacts, senior management, compliance officers
- Committees, auditors, legal advisers

3. Understanding business units:

- For larger organisations, gather information on specific products/services, target clients, income sources, documentation, IT systems, etc.

4. Developing risk management programmes:

- Identify specific responsibilities for each legislative requirement
- Assess impact of legislation on the firm
- Identify key risks and controls
- Develop action plans for weaknesses
- Establish review frequency and overall risk ratings

5. Constructing rules matrices:

- Choose between bottom-up or top-down approach based on firm size/complexity
- Create spreadsheets mapping regulatory handbooks (e.g. SYSC, COBS) to business functions/activities

6. Detailed rules mapping:

- For each relevant law/regulation, determine which parts apply to different sections of the firm
- Identify any gaps or outdated references in existing policies

7. Regular review and updating:

- Continuously reassess and update the rules map as regulations and business activities change

The process aims to systematically identify, organise and manage all applicable regulatory requirements for the firm across its various entities and business units.

Best Practices

There are several industry best practices for rules mapping in financial services compliance:

1. Comprehensive scope:

- Map all applicable regulations, including both financial services-specific and relevant non-financial services regulations
- Cover all jurisdictions where the firm operates
- Include regulations from multiple sources (e.g. local regulators, global bodies)

2. Appropriate granularity:

- Map at both a high level (e.g. overall regulation) and more detailed level (e.g. specific clauses/rules)
- Create plain English summaries of key obligations
- Balance between comprehensive coverage and manageable detail

3. Systematic approach:

- Use a structured methodology, such as spreadsheets or specialized software
- Map regulations to specific business units, functions, processes
- Include key data points like regulatory body, approval dates, etc.

4. Integration with risk and control frameworks:

- Link regulatory requirements to internal policies, procedures and controls

- Identify gaps between regulations and existing controls
- Align with operational risk management processes

5. Regular maintenance:

- Establish processes to monitor regulatory changes
- Update mappings as regulations and business activities evolve

6. Leverage technology:

- Use automation and AI tools to improve efficiency and accuracy
- Implement systems to manage the mapping data and workflow

7. Cross-functional collaboration:

- Involve business units, compliance, legal, risk management
- Clarify roles and responsibilities across first and second lines of defence

8. **Risk-based approach:**

- Prioritise mapping of high-risk or high-impact regulations
- Consider factors like business scale, regulatory focus areas

9. Governance and oversight:

- Establish clear ownership and accountability
- Implement management and board reporting on mapping status

10. Continuous improvement:

- Regularly assess the effectiveness of the mapping process

- Refine approach based on regulatory changes and internal learnings

The key is to implement a systematic, risk-based approach that provides a comprehensive view of regulatory obligations mapped to business activities, while remaining flexible enough to adapt to the evolving regulatory landscape. Leveraging technology and cross-functional collaboration are important enablers for effective rules mapping.

Examples

Some examples of rules mapping in financial services:

1. Regulatory Handbooks to Business Functions Matrix:

A spreadsheet can be created with column headings referencing regulatory handbooks (e.g., SYSC, COBS, BIPRU, INSPRU) and rows representing different business functions or activities (e.g., trading desks, middle office, settlement, life sales, pensions sales, investment sales, mortgages). This matrix helps identify which regulatory handbooks apply to specific areas of the business.

2. Legislation to Internal Policies Mapping:

Financial institutions map internal policies to relevant rules and regulations, including federal rules, stock exchange rules, and Self-Regulating Organisation (SRO) rules. This helps identify potential compliance issues and gaps in policies.

3. Regulatory Requirements to Controls Mapping:

Organisations map specific regulatory requirements to internal controls, policies, and procedures. This helps ensure that appropriate measures are in place to meet each regulatory obligation.

4. Cross-Jurisdictional Regulatory Mapping:

For firms operating in multiple jurisdictions, mapping regulations across different countries or regions to identify commonalities and differences in requirements.

5. Risk-Based Regulatory Mapping:

Mapping regulatory requirements to specific risks within the organisation, helping to prioritise compliance efforts and allocate resources effectively.

6. Process-Based Regulatory Mapping:

Mapping regulations to specific business processes or activities, helping to identify which processes are impacted by particular regulatory requirements.

7. Technology-Enabled Regulatory Mapping:

Using AI and machine learning technologies to automatically map regulatory text to internal policies, procedures, and controls, improving efficiency and accuracy in the mapping process.

8. Compliance Function Operating Model Mapping:

Mapping compliance responsibilities across different areas of expertise (e.g., AML, UDAAP, mortgage compliance) to ensure comprehensive coverage and avoid silos.

9. Third-Party Provider Regulatory Mapping:

Mapping regulatory requirements that apply to third-party service providers and ensuring internal policies and contracts reflect these obligations.

10. Regulatory Change Impact Mapping:

Mapping new or changed regulations to existing policies, procedures, and controls to identify areas requiring updates or new implementations.

These examples demonstrate the various approaches financial services firms can take to map regulatory requirements to their internal structures, processes, and controls, helping to ensure comprehensive compliance management.

Conclusion

Rules mapping is an essential process for compliance managers in the financial services sector. By systematically identifying, organising, and managing regulatory requirements, firms can ensure they remain compliant with the complex and ever-changing regulatory landscape. Regular review and updating of these maps are crucial to maintaining an effective compliance programme.

Chapter 10: Financial Products and Services (including PSD2)

Understanding Financial Products and Services

If you're working as a compliance manager, it's really important to have a complete and detailed understanding of the financial products and services that your company offers. This knowledge is crucial not only because it helps you give sound advice and make better recommendations to your colleagues, but also because it protects you from being tricked by people trying to get inappropriate approvals.

Today, even the smallest retail offices that deal with distribution offer a wide range of financial services products. These include various platforms and packages, plus innovative insurance and mortgage products that have been created since the credit crisis. If you fully understand the regulatory permissions, exemptions, and waivers your company has, it will greatly help you be more effective in your role as a compliance manager.

Knowledge about the products that your firm has recently sold, whether by their specific names or by the type of product they are, is essential to ensure that advisors or teams in the firm stay on track with the strategic goals of the firm. It's important to closely monitor the risk profile of the products, too.

The new business department might not always identify products as high-risk, and they might not be familiar with all the terms and jargon involved.

After you figure out which products are being sold and you understand the sales trends and patterns, it's important to check the latest regulatory positions concerning any unclear areas. The Financial Conduct Authority (FCA) website is a great place to find the most up-to-date consultation papers and policy statements. You can use these resources to support your understanding of regulatory issues.

Retail Distribution Review (RDR) and Service Offerings

The ongoing process of implementing the Retail Distribution Review (RDR) continues to encourage the creation and development of new service offerings designed to address the needs of specific segments of clients. It's very important to understand the level of service each client receives and what fees are involved. Even clients who are transaction-only need to clearly understand that they won't receive ongoing advice.

It's important to communicate clearly about the protections available to consumers regarding the quality and suitability of advice given for any particular transaction.

Some advisors may decide to use an execution-only platform to serve their affluent clients for smaller, recurring transactions, like Individual Savings Accounts (ISAs), to avoid substantial advisory fees.

Keep in mind that such transactions usually do not qualify for Financial Ombudsman Service redress or protection from the Financial Services Compensation Scheme (FSCS), unless the initial advice comes from the advisor or their firm. This highlights the importance of keeping accurate and precise records of all transactions.

Regulated and Unregulated Services

It is essential to distinguish between regulated products and services and those that your firm offers which may not fall under regulation. Some services your company offers might not be regulated by the FCA or the Prudential Regulation Authority (PRA), but they might still be subject to other regulations or laws, such as those governing tax planning, writing wills, and providing unsecured loans, Debt counselling is now regulated by the FCA under the Consumer Credit Act (CCA).

Compliance with Financial Promotions and Documentation

Identifying the financial products your firm offers is one task, but it's also important to consider all aspects related to these products: financial promotions, point-of-sale and post-sale documentation, and the construction of client files, both digital and physical. These files must clearly show compliance with regulatory requirements and may also need to include additional documents, such as those for Anti-Money Laundering (AML) purposes.

There's no need to examine every piece of documentation relating to the sales process thoroughly at this point, but it's crucial to focus primarily on the documentation specifically related to the products themselves.

Regulated Activities

The FCA provides detailed guidelines on specific regulated activities that firms must comply with. These guidelines cover:

- Accepting deposits and issuing electronic money
- Effecting and carrying out contracts of insurance
- Dealing in investments, either as a principal or agent
- Arranging and managing investments
- Providing advice on investments and pension products
- Administering regulated mortgage and insurance contracts
- Offering financial promotions subject to certain conditions

These activities align with the FCA's goals to protect consumers, ensure market integrity, and promote healthy competition within the financial services sector.

Designated Investments

Designated investments, as defined by the FCA, include:

- Securities like shares, debentures, and government and public securities
- Contracts including options, futures, and contracts for differences
- Units in collective investment schemes and stakeholder pension schemes
- Emissions auction products, where applicable

Compliance managers should ensure these designated investments are accurately classified and strictly adhere to all regulatory requirements.

Retail Investment Products (RIPs)

As introduced through the "RETAIL DISTRIBUTION REVIEW (ADVISER CHARGING) INSTRUMENT 2010," Retail Investment Products (RIPs) demand independent advisors who represent themselves as independent to consider and document these specific investment options. RIPs encompass a variety of investments, including:

- Life policies and units
- Stakeholder and personal pension schemes, including group arrangements
- Interests in investment trust savings schemes or securities in investment trusts
- Structured capital-at-risk products

Whether these RIPs are held within an Individual Savings Account (ISA) or a Child Trust Fund (CTF), ensuring comprehensive documentation and effective client advice is essential.

By staying informed about and compliant with these continually changing regulatory standards, you help maintain the integrity of your firm's offerings and reinforce consumer trust in the financial sector as a whole.

Reforms to Financial Services Retail-disclosure Requirements

The Government and FCA announce plans to reform UK retail disclosure rules and will temporarily exempt investment trusts from assimilated EU law requirements.

The Government and FCA are committed to the ongoing reform programme to reinvigorate our capital markets. Ensuring retail investors can make informed investment decisions is an important part of ensuring healthy capital markets. As part of this, the Government and FCA are committed to replacing EU-inherited consumer cost disclosure regulation with a new framework tailored to UK markets and firms.

The Treasury consulted on replacing the EU-inherited Packaged Retail and Insurance-based Investment Products (PRIIPs) Regulation with a new framework for Consumer Composite Investments (CCIs). HM Treasury will lay legislation as soon as possible to provide the FCA with the appropriate powers to deliver this reform. The new CCI regime will deliver more tailored and flexible rules which will address concerns across industry with current disclosure requirements, including for costs.

The UK's new retail disclosure regime is expected to be in place in H1 2025, subject to Parliamentary approval and the FCA consultation process. The FCA intends to consult on proposed rules for the CCI regime this autumn.

The UK's new framework for CCIs will support investors to better understand what they are paying for and the value they are receiving through the distribution chain. The FCA's consultation process will provide an opportunity for a full range of stakeholders to provide feedback on the new regime, to ensure it works as intended.

The intent is that the new CCI framework will be proportionate and will allow more bespoke arrangements to address concerns that have been raised with the current PRIIPs framework.

Payment Services Businesses in the UK

The financial landscape in the UK has undergone significant transformation in recent years, and the payment services sector has been at the forefront of this evolution. As digital technology reshapes how consumers and businesses engage with financial services, understanding the regulatory framework is crucial for compliance professionals. This chapter outlines the key aspects of regulation for payment services businesses under the oversight of the Financial Conduct Authority (FCA).

Regulatory Framework

The Payment Services Directive (PSD2)

Implementing the European Union's Second Payment Services Directive (PSD2), the UK's Payment Services Regulations 2017 brought significant changes. PSD2 aims to enhance competition, innovation, and security within the Single Euro Payments Area (SEPA).

The FCA is responsible for enforcing these regulations, which govern UK payment service providers (PSPs).

FCA's Role and Objectives

The FCA is tasked with ensuring PSPs operate fairly, transparently, and securely. One of its key objectives is to protect consumers and increase the transparency of payment transactions. This involves monitoring firms' compliance with disclosure requirements, consumer rights provisions, and anti-fraud measures.

Authorisation and Registration

Authorisation of Payment Institutions

To operate legally, payment services businesses must either be authorised or registered by the FCA. Authorised Payment Institutions (APIs) are entities permitted to provide payment services as a primary business activity. The authorisation process involves the submission of detailed business plans, governance structures, and proof of financial stability.

Small Payment Institutions (SPIs)

Businesses with lower transaction volumes may opt for registration as Small Payment Institutions (SPIs). SPIs benefit from a lighter supervisory regime but are limited in terms of the scale of operations (e.g., an average monthly transaction volume cap of €3 million).

Regulatory Technical Standards (RTS)

Under PSD2, the European Banking Authority (EBA) developed Regulatory Technical Standards (RTS) on strong customer authentication and secure communication. These standards ensure that APIs and SPIs safeguard users' credentials and reduce fraud risks.

Operational Requirements

Safeguarding Client Funds

Payment institutions are required to protect client funds in the event of insolvency. This usually involves either segregating client monies from business funds or securing them with an insurance policy or similar guarantee.

Conduct of Business Rules

The FCA mandates that firms adhere to conduct rules that ensure transparency and fairness. These include providing clear and concise information on fees, charges, and transaction conditions. Complaints handling and redress mechanisms must also be robust and well-publicised.

Risk Management and Internal Controls

Effective risk management strategies and internal controls are mandatory. These are designed to mitigate risks associated with data breaches, operational failures, and financial crime. Key components often include board oversight, internal audit functions, and compliance checks.

Consumer Protection

Rights and Transparency

PSD2 has strengthened consumer rights, emphasising transparency and reducing liability for unauthorized transactions. Payment institutions must disclose transaction information, including execution times and fees, to consumers in a clear and accessible manner.

Dispute Resolution

The FCA requires that all payment service providers implement mechanisms for addressing customer complaints promptly. Institutions should aim to resolve disputes amicably but have structures in place for escalation if necessary.

Innovation and Competition

Open Banking

One of PSD2's most significant changes is the introduction of Open Banking, which encourages innovative financial products through enhanced data sharing. Through Application Programming Interfaces (APIs), third-party providers can access customer data (with consent) to offer tailored services. This is expected to foster competition and enhance consumer choice.

E-Money and Digital Wallets

Electronic Money Institutions (EMIs) benefit from a separate, albeit overlapping, regulatory framework. EMIs are authorised to issue electronic money, which can be redeemed at par value by the holder. The growth of mobile and digital wallets has brought these institutions to the forefront, necessitating stringent security and anti-fraud measures.

Anti-Money Laundering (AML) and Counter-Terrorist Financing (CTF) Compliance Obligations

Payment services businesses must comply with the UK's Anti-Money Laundering (AML) and Counter-Terrorist Financing (CTF) regulations. This involves customer due diligence, transaction monitoring, and reporting suspicious activities to the National Crime Agency (NCA).

Know Your Customer (KYC)

Adequate KYC procedures are essential for verifying customer identities and mitigating financial crime risks. The FCA expects firms to maintain robust KYC measures and regularly update customer information as part of ongoing monitoring.

Emerging Trends and Challenges

Cybersecurity

The increasing digitalisation of payment services brings heightened cybersecurity risks. Institutions must adopt advanced technologies and continually update security protocols to safeguard against cyber threats and data breaches.

Regulatory Developments Post-Brexit

Since Brexit, the UK has been adapting its regulatory framework independently of the EU. While maintaining high standards, the FCA aims to provide greater flexibility and proportionality in regulation. Firms must stay informed of these evolving regulatory landscapes.

Conclusion

The regulatory environment for payment services businesses in the UK is complex and dynamic. To maintain compliance and protect consumer interests, firms must understand the intricacies of the Financial Conduct Authority's requirements. With continued advancements in technology and shifts in consumer behaviour, the payment services sector is poised for further innovation and evolution.

Keeping abreast of regulatory changes and adopting a proactive approach to compliance will be vital for success in this field.

For a comprehensive understanding of the FCA's approach to regulating payment services and electronic money, refer to the official guidance document at FCA's Approach to Payment Services and Electronic Money 2017.

Chapter 11: Compliance in Support Functions

The importance of regulatory compliance across all areas of a firm cannot be overstated. In today's financial landscape, where regulations are continually evolving, a firm must ensure that compliance is embedded in every facet of its operations. This chapter explores the role of compliance in support functions and provides guidance on how each department within a firm can maintain and promote regulatory adherence.

Understanding Compliance in Different Roles

Compliance is not the sole responsibility of a dedicated team or individual; rather, it is a firm-wide concern that touches every role from the executive team down to part-time or temporary staff. While the depth of knowledge required may vary depending on the responsibilities of each role, it is crucial that everyone is aware of how compliance impacts their duties and the firm at large.

For example, senior management, such as directors or business principals, need to have a comprehensive understanding of specific compliance requirements related to their roles. This includes an awareness of governance and conduct expectations as per the Financial Conduct Authority (FCA) norms. The FCA's Senior Managers and Certification Regime (SMCR) underscores the need for leadership to take ownership of their compliance obligations.

Tailored Training and Information Dissemination

The responsibility of training and ensuring compliance awareness typically falls on the compliance manager. Training methods should be diverse and adaptable to the needs of different staff members and departments. This may include:

- **In-house seminars and workshops**: These provide interactive opportunities for staff to engage with compliance topics relevant to their functions.
- **Online training modules**: An efficient way to deliver consistent training across multiple locations.
- **External courses and certifications**: These may be particularly beneficial for senior staff needing advanced or specialised knowledge.
- **Regular compliance updates**: Through circulars or memos that address recent regulatory changes, keeping staff informed.

An annual training schedule can help facilitate this, alongside a requirement for employees to attest to their understanding of compliance obligations. Missing such requirements should trigger a review or disciplinary process to ensure standards are maintained.

Embedding Compliance within Corporate Culture

Firms often develop a unique culture, especially if they have begun from humble beginnings.

However, cultivating a culture of compliance is crucial. It is the role of the compliance manager to ensure that all staff share and understand the firm's compliance ethos.

Proper management of this cultural integration is key to avoiding regulatory failings, which can lead to pressures not only internally but from regulators as well.

In recent years, the FCA has increased its focus on governance, risk management, and culture within firms. They expect businesses to operate with a strong ethical backbone rather than merely acting as "financial sales houses." It's essential for senior management to enable a compliance-focused culture by leading by example.

Key Regulatory Responsibilities

The scale of regulatory responsibilities that a firm must manage is vast and includes, but is not limited to:

- **Apportionment and oversight**: Ensuring all staff understand their regulatory responsibilities, particularly those in management roles.
- **Chinese walls**: Where appropriate, maintaining internal information barriers to prevent conflicts of interest.
- **Data protection**: Complying with the General Data Protection Regulation (GDPR) to safeguard personal data.

- **Insider dealing**: Preventing the misuse of confidential information and ensuring all actions align with the Market Abuse Regulation (MAR).
- **Company announcements**: Ensuring accuracy and regulatory compliance in all public communications.
- **Complaints handling and training**: Maintaining robust processes to manage and learn from complaints effectively.

Moreover, the SMCR places emphasis on individual accountability, with the senior persons within a firm held accountable for breaches within their areas.

Managing Support Functions

A firm's operations are often divided into front and back office, where compliance requirements may differ. The front office typically manages customer interactions, while the back office maintains support functions crucial for operational efficiency.

It's essential that the compliance team works closely with both departments to ensure they have the necessary tools and understanding to meet their regulatory requirements. Any lack of compliance understanding or gaps in regulatory procedures can create significant risks for the firm.

Continuous Improvement

Regulatory compliance is not a one-time effort but requires continual improvement and adaptation to changing regulatory landscapes.

As such, having robust Management Information (MI) systems can support senior managers in monitoring compliance performance and in identifying areas for enhancement.

Finally, proactive engagement with the FCA through open communication and transparency can foster a positive regulatory relationship, aiding in the firm's ongoing compliance journey. Ultimately, compliance should be viewed not only as a regulatory obligation but as a cornerstone of the firm's operational integrity and client trustworthiness.

The Three Lines of Defence Model

In the realm of financial regulatory compliance, particularly within UK financial firms, the "Three Lines of Defence" model is a widely recognized framework designed to ensure effective risk management and control. This model delineates responsibilities and roles across the organisation, ensuring that risks are adequately managed, and governance processes are upheld. It is vital for firms, especially in the support functions ties to regulatory compliance, to understand and implement this model effectively.

First Line of Defence: Operational Management

The first line of defence is composed of the business units and operational management. These are the individuals and teams responsible for owning and managing risk directly. Their primary role includes:

- **Risk Control Implementation**: Executing day-to-day activities that identify and manage potential risks.
- **Policy Adherence**: Ensuring that all operational activities comply with established internal policies and standards, including those set by the FCA and other regulatory bodies.
- **Cultural Integration**: Promoting a culture of compliance and risk awareness throughout their teams to proactively manage risks as they arise.

Support functions in the first line are integral in ensuring that processes align with regulatory requirements, and they often conduct initial assessments and monitoring to prevent compliance breaches.

Second Line of Defence: Risk Management and Compliance Functions

The second line provides oversight and facilitation. It comprises dedicated compliance and risk management teams tasked with the following:

- **Framework Development**: Establishing the policies, frameworks, and tools necessary for risk management, ensuring they are robust and comprehensive.
- **Independent Monitoring and Reporting**: Conducting ongoing monitoring to ensure that risk controls are effective and compliance is maintained. This includes reporting on risk exposures and compliance status to senior management.

- **Guidance and Support**: Offering expertise and advisory services to the first line on risk and compliance issues. They play a crucial role in interpreting regulatory requirements, such as those from the FCA, and translating them into actionable plans for operational management.

These functions act as a bridge between operational activities and strategic oversight, ensuring that compliance efforts are aligned with the firm's risk appetite and regulatory expectations.

Third Line of Defence: Internal Audit

The third line is independent assurance. This role is typically fulfilled by internal audit functions which have a mandate to:

- **Objective Assurance**: Conduct independent audits to evaluate the effectiveness of the first and second lines of defence. This involves assessing the design and operation of risk management, control, and governance processes.
- **Recommendations for Improvement**: Providing insights and recommendations to enhance the risk management framework and ensure compliance with standards.
- **Accountability Assurance**: Reporting to the highest levels of the organisation, including the Board, to ensure accountability and transparency in risk management processes.

Incorporating the third line of defence serves as a crucial checkpoint to guarantee that the organisation's compliance and risk management efforts are effective and evolving in response to regulatory changes and internal developments.

Three Lines of Defence – in more detail

The first line of defence in the Three Lines of Defence model refers to the business operations and support functions that directly own and manage risks within an organisation. Here's a more detailed explanation of the first line of defence:

First Line of Defence: Business Operations

The first line of defence comprises the frontline staff and operational management who are responsible for the day-to-day running of the business. Their key responsibilities include:

1. **Risk Ownership**: They are the primary owners and managers of risks within their areas of operation.

2. **Risk Identification**: They are responsible for identifying potential risks in their daily activities and processes.

3. **Control Implementation**: They design and implement internal controls to mitigate identified risks.

4. **Policy Compliance**: They ensure adherence to internal policies, procedures, and regulatory requirements.

5. **Reporting**: They report on the effectiveness of controls and any risk incidents to management.

6. **Risk Assessment**: They conduct regular risk assessments within their areas of responsibility.

7. **Training**: They participate in and sometimes deliver compliance and risk management training relevant to their roles.

8. **Customer Interaction**: In financial services, the first line often includes those who directly interact with customers, ensuring compliance with conduct rules and treating customers fairly principles.

9. **Data Management**: They are responsible for maintaining accurate and complete data, which is crucial for regulatory reporting and risk management.

10. **Escalation**: They escalate any compliance concerns or potential breaches to the appropriate channels, including the second line of defence.

The first line of defence plays a crucial role in embedding a culture of compliance and risk awareness throughout the organisation. Their proximity to the day-to-day operations makes them the first point of detection and prevention for many risks and compliance issues.

Effective risk management at this level can significantly reduce the organisation's overall risk exposure and strengthen its compliance posture.

The second line of defence in the Three Lines of Defence model refers to the risk management and compliance functions within an organisation. Here's a detailed explanation of the second line of defence:

Second Line of Defence: Risk Management and Compliance Functions

The second line of defence provides oversight, support, and challenge to the first line. It typically includes specialised functions such as:

1. **Risk Management**: Responsible for developing and maintaining the risk management framework.

2. **Compliance**: Ensures adherence to laws, regulations, and internal policies.

3. **Financial Control**: Oversees financial risks and controls.

4. **Security**: Manages information and physical security risks.

5. **Quality Assurance**: Ensures quality standards are met across the organisation.

Key responsibilities of the second line include:

1. **Policy Development**: Creating and maintaining risk management and compliance policies and procedures.

2. **Risk Monitoring**: Overseeing the implementation of risk management practices across the organisation.

3. **Compliance Monitoring**: Conducting reviews to ensure adherence to regulatory requirements and internal policies.

4. **Reporting**: Providing regular risk and compliance reports to senior management and the board.

5. **Training and Guidance**: Offering training and advice to the first line on risk and compliance matters.

6. **Challenge Function**: Providing constructive challenge to the first line's risk assessments and control measures.

7. **Regulatory Liaison**: Acting as a point of contact with regulators and interpreting regulatory changes.

8. **Risk Aggregation**: Consolidating risk information from across the organisation to provide a holistic view.

9. Incident Management: Supporting the first line in managing and reporting risk incidents.

10. Control Testing: Independently testing the effectiveness of controls implemented by the first line.

The second line of defence plays a crucial role in supporting the organisation's risk management strategy and ensuring that compliance is embedded throughout the business. It acts as a bridge between the operational first line and the assurance-providing third line, helping to maintain a robust risk and compliance framework.

The third line of defence in the Three Lines of Defence model is typically represented by the Internal Audit function. Here's a detailed explanation of the third line of defence:

Third Line of Defence: Internal Audit

The third line of defence provides independent assurance to the board and senior management on the effectiveness of the first and second lines. Key aspects of the third line include:

1. Independence: Internal Audit operates independently from both the first and second lines, reporting directly to the board or audit committee.

2. Objective Assurance: It provides an unbiased and objective view of the organisation's risk management, governance, and internal control processes.

3. Risk-Based Approach: Internal Audit typically uses a risk-based methodology to prioritise its activities.

4. Comprehensive Coverage: It reviews all aspects of the organisation, including the activities of the first and second lines of defence.

5. Evaluation of Controls: Assesses the design and effectiveness of controls implemented by the first and second lines.

6. Recommendations: Provides recommendations for improvement in processes and controls.

Key responsibilities of the third line include:

1. Auditing: Conducting regular audits of various business units, processes, and systems.

2. Assessing Effectiveness: Evaluating the effectiveness of risk management and compliance functions (second line).

3. Reporting: Providing detailed reports to the board and senior management on audit findings and recommendations.

4. Follow-up: Monitoring the implementation of agreed actions from previous audits.

5. Advisory Role: Offering insights on emerging risks and best practices in risk management and control.

6. Coordination: Working with external auditors and regulators to ensure comprehensive coverage and avoid duplication of efforts.

7. Quality Assurance: Maintaining its own quality assurance and improvement programme.

8. Fraud Investigation: Often tasked with leading or supporting fraud investigations.

The third line of defence plays a crucial role in providing assurance to stakeholders that the organisation's risk management and internal control processes are operating effectively. It serves as the last internal check before external auditors or regulators review the organisation's practices.

The Three Lines of Defence model is a fundamental concept in modern risk management and compliance frameworks, complementing the comprehensive approach to compliance in support functions described in the chapter.

Integrating the Model in Financial Compliance Strategy

For support functions, understanding and applying the three lines of defence model is instrumental in achieving robust financial regulatory compliance. It affords a structured approach to managing risks and fulfilling compliance obligations under current FCA regulations and other relevant standards. Integration of this model ensures that communication channels, accountability, and oversight mechanisms are firmly in place, hence promoting an organisation-wide culture of compliance and proactive risk management.

Incorporating these structured lines not only aids in compliance but also positions financial firms to navigate the ever-evolving regulatory landscape with confidence and agility.

Chapter 12: Regular Compliance Activities

In the ever-evolving landscape of financial services regulation, the role of the Compliance Manager remains crucial. This chapter focuses on the essential regular compliance activities that form the backbone of a robust compliance regime. While the specifics may vary depending on the firm's size and nature of business, the core principles and activities discussed here are broadly applicable across the industry.

Compliance Culture and Ethics

The foundation of any effective compliance programme is a strong culture of ethics and compliance within the organisation. This goes beyond mere rule-following and extends to fostering an environment where ethical behaviour is ingrained in every aspect of the business.

Objective: To cultivate a corporate culture that consistently promotes ethical business practices and fair treatment of customers.

Implementation:

Instilling a compliance-focused mindset requires more than just policies and training. It demands a commitment from the top down, with senior management setting the tone and leading by example.

The Compliance Manager plays a pivotal role as the ethical compass of the organisation, supported by senior leadership who reinforce the importance of compliance at every opportunity.

Consider establishing an ethics committee to discuss plans and changes from a moral perspective and address any areas requiring disciplinary or corrective action. This committee can serve as a forum for open dialogue about ethical dilemmas and reputational risks.

Many professional bodies now require ethics modules as part of their qualifications. Encouraging staff to pursue these qualifications or providing in-house ethics training can help reinforce the importance of ethical behaviour in financial services.

Maintaining A Compliance Manual

While not a strict regulatory requirement, maintaining a comprehensive compliance manual is generally expected by regulators and serves as a crucial reference point for staff.

Objective: To provide a centralised resource that outlines regulatory requirements, internal policies, and procedures for staff to reference.

Implementation:

The compliance manual should cover:

1. The purpose and importance of compliance
2. A description of the compliance function and the Compliance Manager's responsibilities
3. The firm's regulatory permissions and any specific exemptions or variations
4. Relevant regulatory requirements and their impact on staff roles
5. Guidance on how staff can comply with rules in their daily duties
6. Potential penalties for non-compliance
7. References to other internal policies and external sources of information

Consider hosting the manual on a cloud-based platform or intranet for easy access and updates. Implement an annual attestation process where staff confirm they have read, understood, and agree to comply with the manual.

Reviewing Policies and Procedures

Regular review and updating of policies and procedures ensure they remain relevant and effective in the face of regulatory changes and evolving business practices.

Objective: To maintain up-to-date policies and procedures that provide clear guidance and set appropriate parameters for staff.

Implementation:

Identify all mandatory policies required by the Financial Conduct Authority (FCA), such as those outlined in the Systems and Controls (SYSC) sourcebook, including conflict of interest, customer complaints, anti-money laundering (AML), counter-terrorist financing (CTF), whistleblowing, and data security policies.

Establish a policy approval process, typically involving board approval for significant changes. Use version control and update logs to track changes. Consider assigning individual responsibility for maintaining specific policies to ensure timely updates.

Include policy reviews in your annual compliance monitoring plan to ensure regular assessment and updating.

Regulatory Training

Ongoing training is essential to ensure all staff are aware of their compliance responsibilities and remain up-to-date with regulatory requirements.

Objective: To equip staff with the knowledge and understanding necessary to fulfil their compliance obligations effectively.

Implementation:

Identify training needs based on regulatory requirements, internal risk assessments, and changes in the business or regulatory landscape. Consider a mix of training methods, including:

- External training providers for specialist topics
- Online training modules with assessment components
- Regular regulatory update emails or bulletins
- Workshops or presentations by the Compliance team
- External courses for specific roles or senior staff

Ensure training is tailored to different roles within the organisation and maintain accurate records of attendance and completion. Follow up with those who miss training sessions and escalate persistent non-attendance to senior management.

Compliance Monitoring Plan

A well-structured compliance monitoring plan is crucial for systematically assessing the effectiveness of the firm's compliance controls and identifying areas for improvement.

Objective: To provide a comprehensive framework for testing and evaluating compliance across all relevant areas of the business.

Implementation:

Develop an annual compliance monitoring plan that covers all key risk areas identified through your firm's risk assessment process. The plan should include:

1. Areas to be reviewed
2. Frequency of reviews

3. Methodology for each review
4. Responsible individuals
5. Reporting mechanisms

Ensure the plan is flexible enough to accommodate ad hoc reviews in response to emerging risks or regulatory changes. Present the plan to the board or risk committee for approval and provide regular updates on its progress throughout the year.

Regulatory Reporting

Timely and accurate regulatory reporting is a fundamental compliance obligation for all regulated firms.

Objective: To ensure all required regulatory reports are submitted accurately and on time.

Implementation:

Maintain a comprehensive calendar of regulatory reporting deadlines, including:

- Financial reports (e.g., COREP, FINREP for applicable firms)
- Conduct of Business reports (e.g., RMAR for retail investment firms)
- Ad hoc reports required by the FCA

Establish clear processes for data gathering, validation, and sign-off for each report. Consider implementing automated reporting solutions where possible to reduce the risk of errors and improve efficiency.

Managing Regulatory Change

Staying abreast of regulatory developments and implementing necessary changes is a critical ongoing activity for the Compliance function.

Objective: To ensure the firm remains compliant with evolving regulatory requirements and adapts its practices accordingly.

Implementation:

1. Subscribe to FCA updates and industry newsletters
2. Regularly review the FCA's Business Plan and other strategic documents
3. Participate in industry forums and working groups
4. Maintain a regulatory change log to track upcoming changes and their impact on the firm
5. Develop implementation plans for significant regulatory changes, involving relevant business areas and senior management

Consider using regulatory technology (RegTech) solutions to help monitor and manage regulatory change more efficiently.

Conflicts of Interest Management

Effectively managing conflicts of interest is crucial for maintaining trust and integrity in financial services.

Objective: To identify, prevent, and manage conflicts of interest that could adversely affect clients or the firm's reputation.

Implementation:

1. Maintain and regularly update a conflicts of interest register
2. Conduct annual reviews of potential conflicts across all business areas
3. Implement robust policies and procedures for identifying and managing conflicts
4. Provide regular training to staff on recognising and handling conflicts of interest
5. Ensure appropriate disclosure to clients where conflicts cannot be fully mitigated

Review and update the conflicts of interest policy at least annually, seeking board approval for any significant changes.

Anti-Money Laundering (AML) and Counter-Terrorist Financing (CTF)

Robust AML and CTF controls are essential for protecting the firm and the wider financial system from financial crime.

Objective: To prevent the firm from being used for money laundering or terrorist financing purposes.

Implementation:

1. Maintain up-to-date AML and CTF policies and procedures
2. Conduct regular risk assessments of the firm's exposure to money laundering and terrorist financing risks
3. Implement and regularly review customer due diligence processes
4. Provide ongoing AML training to all staff, with enhanced training for high-risk roles
5. Maintain effective transaction monitoring systems
6. Ensure prompt reporting of suspicious activity to the National Crime Agency

The Money Laundering Reporting Officer (MLRO) should provide an annual report to the board on the effectiveness of the firm's AML controls.

Data Protection and Cybersecurity

With the increasing importance of data protection and the growing threat of cyber-attacks, compliance activities in this area have become critical.

Objective: To ensure compliance with data protection regulations and maintain robust cybersecurity defences.

Implementation:

1. Maintain and regularly update data protection policies and procedures
2. Conduct regular data protection impact assessments
3. Provide ongoing training on data protection and cybersecurity best practices
4. Implement and test incident response plans for data breaches
5. Regularly review and update cybersecurity measures
6. Ensure proper oversight of any third-party data processors

Consider appointing a Data Protection Officer if required under the UK General Data Protection Regulation (GDPR).

Common Pitfalls in Compliance Manual Maintenance

Some common pitfalls to avoid when maintaining a compliance manual include:

1. Not keeping it up-to-date: The manual needs to be regularly reviewed and updated to reflect regulatory changes and evolving business practices.

2. Making it inaccessible: Locating the manual on paper copies in different departments can make it difficult to access and update. It's better to have it on an intranet or cloud service for easy access and updates.

3. Lack of version control: Not using proper version control and update logs can make it hard to track changes over time.

4. Not getting staff attestation: Failing to have staff attest annually that they have read, understood and agree to comply with the manual.

5. Insufficient content: The manual should comprehensively cover key areas like the purpose of compliance, description of the compliance function, regulatory permissions, relevant requirements, guidance for staff, and potential penalties.

6. Not linking to other policies: Failing to use the compliance manual as a central hub to reference other associated policies and procedures.

7. Lack of board approval: Not having a proper approval process, including board approval for significant changes.

8. Overlooking training needs: Not using the manual as a basis for identifying and addressing staff training needs on compliance topics.

9. Treating it as a static document: Viewing the manual as a one-time effort rather than a living document that requires ongoing maintenance.

10. Not tailoring it to the firm: Using a generic manual without adapting it sufficiently to the specific needs and regulatory requirements of the firm.

Compliance Challenges for Small & Medium Sized Firms

Here are some critical tips regarding how small and medium-sized firms can address compliance challenges:

1. Foster a strong compliance culture and ethics from the top down. The Compliance Manager should act as an ethical compass, supported by senior management reinforcing the importance of compliance.

2. Maintain a comprehensive and up-to-date compliance manual that is easily accessible to all staff, preferably on an intranet or cloud service. Have staff attest annually that they have read and understood it.

3. Regularly review and update policies and procedures to ensure they remain relevant. Establish a policy approval process, typically involving board approval for significant changes.

4. Implement a robust regulatory training programme tailored to different roles within the organisation. Use a mix of methods like external providers, online modules, workshops, and presentations by the Compliance team.

5. Develop an annual compliance monitoring plan that systematically assesses the effectiveness of compliance controls across all key risk areas.

6. Stay abreast of regulatory developments through FCA updates, industry newsletters, and participation in industry forums. Maintain a regulatory change log to track upcoming changes.

7. Effectively manage conflicts of interest by maintaining and regularly updating a conflicts of interest register, conducting annual reviews, and providing staff training on the topic.

8. Implement robust anti-money laundering (AML) and counter-terrorist financing (CTF) controls, including regular risk assessments and staff training.

9. Prioritise data protection and cybersecurity measures, including regular impact assessments and incident response plans.

10. Consider using regulatory technology (RegTech) solutions to help monitor and manage regulatory change more efficiently, especially for resource-constrained smaller firms.

11. For areas where internal expertise may be lacking, consider engaging external consultants or compliance services to provide additional support and a fresh perspective on compliance processes.

By focusing on these areas, small and medium-sized firms can build a robust compliance framework that is proportionate to their size and nature of business while meeting regulatory expectations.

How Can Senior Management Support the Compliance Culture?

Senior Management plays a crucial role in fostering a strong compliance culture within a firm:

1. **Setting the tone from the top:** The chapter emphasizes that leaders need to set the "tone from the top" when it comes to instilling a compliance culture and ethics in the organisation.

2. **Supporting the Compliance Manager:** Senior management should support the Compliance Manager, who acts as an "ethical and moral compass" for the firm. The Compliance Manager needs backing from senior leaders to be effective in this role.

3. **Reinforcing compliance importance:** Senior management should "reinforce and recommend the required culture changes at every opportunity". This ongoing reinforcement from leadership is key to embedding compliance into the organisational culture.

4. **Approving policies:** The board or senior management is typically responsible for approving significant changes to compliance policies and procedures.

5. **Addressing non-compliance:** The chapter mentions that persistent non-attendance at compliance training should be reported to senior management, implying they have a role in addressing compliance failures.

6. **Supporting training initiatives**: While not explicitly stated, the chapter implies that senior management should provide support for compliance training programs and initiatives.

7. **Ethical leadership:** By acting ethically themselves and promoting ethical Behaviour, senior leaders help create an environment where compliance is valued.

In essence, senior management's active involvement and visible commitment to compliance is crucial for creating a strong compliance culture throughout the organisation. Their actions and priorities set the standard for the rest of the firm to follow.

Measuring Effectiveness of Compliance Programs

Here are typical ways firms can measure the effectiveness of their compliance programs:

1. **Compliance monitoring plan**: Develop and implement an annual compliance monitoring plan that systematically assesses the effectiveness of compliance controls across all key risk areas. This provides a structured framework for testing and evaluating compliance.

2. **Regular policy and procedure reviews**: Conduct regular reviews of policies and procedures to ensure they remain up-to-date and effective. This can help identify gaps or areas for improvement.

3. **Training completion and assessment**: Track completion rates of compliance training programs and assess staff understanding through tests or practical application. This measures how well staff are absorbing compliance knowledge.

4. **Attestation process**: Implement an annual attestation process where staff confirm they have read, understood, and agree to comply with the compliance manual and key policies. This gauges staff awareness and commitment.

5. **Incident tracking**: Monitor and analyse compliance incidents, breaches, or near-misses. Tracking these over time can indicate the effectiveness of controls and highlight areas needing attention.

6. **Internal audit findings**: Review findings from internal audits related to compliance areas. This provides an independent assessment of compliance program effectiveness.

7. **Regulatory reporting accuracy**: Assess the timeliness and accuracy of regulatory reporting. Consistent, error-free reporting can indicate effective compliance processes.

8. **Customer complaints**: Monitor the volume and nature of customer complaints related to compliance issues. A reduction in such complaints may indicate improved compliance.

9. **Regulatory examination results**: Review feedback and findings from regulatory examinations or visits. Improvements in these results over time can indicate an effective compliance program.

10. **Staff feedback:** Gather feedback from staff on the clarity and practicality of compliance policies and procedures. This can help identify areas where the program may be falling short in day-to-day application.

11. **Benchmarking**: Compare your compliance program and outcomes against industry peers or best practices to identify areas for improvement.

By using a combination of these measures, firms can gain a comprehensive view of their compliance program's effectiveness and identify areas for continuous improvement.

How does Technology & Automation Help Smaller Firms?

Based on the information provided in the attached chapter, technology and automation can play several important roles in compliance for small firms:

1. **Compliance manual accessibility**: Locating the compliance manual on an intranet or cloud service (like Windows Live) makes it easier to maintain and provide access to staff. This allows for easier updates and informing staff of changes.

2. **Policy and procedure management**: While not explicitly stated, the emphasis on maintaining up-to-date policies and procedures suggests that document management systems or policy management software could be beneficial for version control and distribution*.

3. **Training delivery**: Online training and testing as one method for delivering regulatory training to staff. This suggests that e-learning platforms or learning management systems* could be useful for small firms.

4. **Record keeping**: The importance of accurately recording training attendance and following up with absentees implies that automated tracking systems could be helpful.

5. **Regulatory reporting**: While not discussed in detail earlier, regulatory reporting as a compliance activity. Automated reporting tools could help ensure accuracy and timeliness of submissions.

6. **Monitoring regulatory changes**: The need to stay updated on regulatory developments suggests that regulatory intelligence tools or automated alert systems could be valuable*.

7. **Compliance monitoring**: The emphasis on regular testing of compliance controls suggests that automated monitoring and testing tools could be beneficial*.

8. **Risk management**: The mention of maintaining a compliance and regulatory risks register implies that risk management software could be useful*.

**Compliance Consultant has options and the latest systems available for use. Just ask.*

It's clear that various aspects of compliance management could benefit from automation, especially for resource-constrained smaller firms. However, it's important to note that technology should complement, not replace, the human judgment and oversight provided by the Compliance Manager and team.

In conclusion, these regular compliance activities form the core of a robust compliance programme. While the specific implementation may vary depending on the firm's size and nature of business, these activities provide a solid foundation for maintaining regulatory compliance and fostering a strong compliance culture.

As the regulatory landscape continues to evolve, so too must the Compliance Manager's approach to these activities, always staying alert to new requirements and best practices in the field.

Chapter 13: Compliance Advisory Work

In the realm of regulatory compliance, the role of advisory work cannot be overstated. Despite the myriad responsibilities that compliance professionals juggle, there must always be room for providing guidance and counsel to colleagues and stakeholders.

The Essence of Compliance Advisory

Compliance advisory work is a multifaceted role that combines expertise, empathy, and mentorship. It involves being a repository of knowledge, a confidant, and a guiding force within an organisation. To effectively manage this crucial aspect of compliance, it is advisable to maintain an advice log. This log should meticulously record:

- Enquiry method
- Person making the enquiry
- Specific area of concern
- Detailed query
- Relevant rules and regulations
- Response provided
- Time taken to address the query
- Any specific conditions
- Links to relevant correspondence

This systematic approach serves multiple purposes. It ensures consistency in responses, provides justification for advice given, and offers a clear record of the compliance department's activities and workload.

The Four-Stage Advisory Process

When approaching compliance advisory work, a structured four-stage process can be immensely helpful:

1. **Gather comprehensive details**: Collect all pertinent facts related to the query.
2. **Ensure thorough understanding**: Clarify any ambiguities before proceeding.
3. **Assess regulatory impacts**: Determine the potential regulatory consequences of any decision.
4. **Formulate and deliver the response**: Provide a final answer, including any necessary caveats or requirements, and escalate if additional authority is needed.

The Six Honest Serving-Men

Drawing inspiration from Rudyard Kipling's poem, compliance professionals can benefit from employing the "six honest serving-men" methodology to fully comprehend and address queries:

What

- What exactly does the query entail?
- Is it regarding a new service or product?

- Which legislation is relevant?

Why

- What circumstances led to this query?
- Why are existing processes inadequate?
- Why is a timely response crucial?

When

- What is the timeline for implementation or has action already been taken?
- Are there any timing considerations (e.g., tax implications, financial year-end)?

How

- How will the outcome impact the firm?
- Will policy changes be necessary?
- How will this affect existing processes?

Who

- Which internal stakeholders are involved?
- What type of client is affected?
- Which regulatory body might be concerned?

Where

- Which jurisdiction applies?
- Where are the clients based (residence and domicile)?
- Where will the decision have the most significant impact?

Best Practices in Advisory Work

To ensure effective compliance advisory work, consider the following best practices:

1. **Request written queries**: Encourage colleagues to submit queries in writing, providing time for considered responses and maintaining an audit trail.

2. **Utilise an advice log**: Implement a comprehensive log to record all enquiries, responses, and relevant documentation.

3. **Seek clarification**: Don't hesitate to ask for additional information from the query originator or other relevant parties.

4. **Consult widely**: Engage with compliance colleagues, industry associations, or other departments when necessary.

5. **Check definitions and rules**: Always verify definitions, glossaries, and relevant regulations before responding.

6. **Consider multiple contexts**: Examine the query from various angles to ensure a comprehensive response.

7. **Use reliable references**: Utilise authoritative sources such as the Oxford English Dictionary and internal policy documents

Categories of Compliance Queries

Compliance queries can span a wide range of topics. A non-exhaustive list of categories to consider for your advice log might include:

- Regulatory approval
- Staff authorisation
- Threshold conditions
- Fitness and propriety
- Complaints handling
- Conduct risk
- Regulatory breaches
- Anti-money laundering (AML)
- Conflicts of interest
- Fraud prevention
- Outsourcing
- Rules and guidance interpretation
- Data security
- Technology risks
- Operational losses
- Regulatory reporting
- Regulatory notifications
- Regulatory capital requirements
- Acquisitions
- Client asset protection
- Business continuity and disaster recovery
- Documentation requirements
- Regulatory sanctions

- Financial promotions
- Policies and procedures
- General enquiries

Post-Response Considerations

After addressing a query, it's crucial to reflect on any broader implications or necessary follow-up actions:

- **Policies and procedures**: Assess whether new or revised policies are needed to prevent similar issues in the future.

- **Disciplinary action**: Determine if any disciplinary measures are required, consulting with Human Resources as necessary.

- **Notifications**: Identify any stakeholders, regulators, or internal management who should be informed of the situation.

- **Outsourcing agreements**: Evaluate whether any outsourcing arrangements have failed to meet expectations and consider invoking exit strategies if necessary.

- **Disaster recovery and business continuity**: Assess whether the situation warrants invoking disaster recovery or business continuity plans, or if these plans need revision.

- **Training and competence**: Identify any skill gaps or training needs highlighted by the query.

- **Governance**: Consider whether recurring issues necessitate the formation of a dedicated committee or forum.

- **Internal procedures**: If similar queries arise frequently, develop standardised frameworks or templates to streamline the response process.

The Bigger Picture

When grappling with complex compliance queries, it's essential to consider the broader implications:

- Does the proposed action or decision pass the "smell test"?
- Would you be comfortable seeing it reported in the Financial Times?
- How would you explain the decision to a regulator?
- If widely adopted, would this practice have a positive or negative impact on the financial services industry?

If an issue cannot be resolved internally, consider:

1. Approaching your trade body to gauge industry-wide sentiment
2. Contacting the regulator directly through their helpline
3. Reserving the issue for inclusion in a future consultation paper response

Consistency in Response

To ensure consistency in your compliance advisory responses, consider implementing the following best practices:

1. **Maintain a comprehensive advice log:** Record all enquiries, responses, and relevant details in a structured format. This log should include:

    - Enquiry method
    - Person making the enquiry
    - Specific area of concern
    - Detailed query
    - Relevant rules and regulations
    - Response provided
    - Time taken to address the query
    - Any specific conditions
    - Links to relevant correspondence

2. **Follow a structured advisory process**: Adopt a four-stage approach to handling queries:

- Gather comprehensive details
- Ensure thorough understanding
- Assess regulatory impacts
- Formulate and deliver the response

3. **Use the "six honest serving-men" methodology**: Apply this approach to fully comprehend and address queries by considering the What, Why, When, How, Who, and Where of each situation.

4. **Develop standardised frameworks or templates**: For frequently asked questions or similar types of enquiries, create consistent response formats to streamline the process.

5. **Regularly review and update your knowledge**: Stay informed about regulatory changes, industry trends, and best practices to ensure your advice remains current and accurate.

6. **Consult with colleagues and experts:** When faced with complex queries, seek input from other compliance professionals, industry associations, or relevant departments within your organisation.

7. **Document your reasoning:** Clearly explain the rationale behind your advice, citing relevant rules, regulations, and internal policies.

8. **Conduct periodic reviews of past advice:** Regularly assess your previous responses to ensure they remain valid and consistent with current regulations and company policies.

9. **Utilise reliable reference materials**: Consistently refer to authoritative sources such as regulatory handbooks, internal policy documents, and industry guidelines.

10. **Implement a peer review process:** For complex or high-impact queries, consider having another compliance professional review your response before issuing it.

11. **Maintain a centralised knowledge base:** Create and regularly update a repository of common queries and their standard responses, accessible to all compliance team members.

By implementing these practices, you can significantly improve the consistency and quality of your compliance advisory responses, ensuring that your guidance remains reliable and aligned with regulatory requirements and company policies.

Advice Log Best Practices

Here are the best practices for maintaining an advice log in compliance advisory work:

1. Record comprehensive details: Include the following information for each query:

- Enquiry method
- Person making the enquiry
- Specific area of concern

- Detailed query
- Relevant rules and regulations
- Response provided
- Time taken to address the query
- Any specific conditions
- Hyperlinks to relevant correspondence

2. Categorise queries: Develop a robust categorisation system for compliance queries. Some suggested categories include:

- Regulatory approval
- Staff authorisation
- Threshold conditions
- Fitness and propriety
- Complaints handling
- Conduct risk
- Regulatory breaches
- Anti-money laundering (AML)
- Conflicts of interest
- Fraud prevention
- Outsourcing
- Rules and guidance interpretation

3. Ensure consistency: Use the advice log to maintain consistency in responses to similar queries.

4. Justify advice: Keep a record of the rationale behind your advice and any references used.

5. Track time and activity: Record the time taken to address each query to demonstrate the level of activity within the compliance department.

6. Maintain an audit trail: Use the log to provide evidence that queries were dealt with and in what timescale.

7. Identify training needs: Analyse the log to identify commonly asked questions, which can indicate areas where additional compliance training may be needed.

8. Facilitate easy retrieval: Organise the log in a way that allows for quick and easy access to past advice when needed.

9. Include hyperlinks: Add links to relevant documentation or emails for each query to provide a comprehensive record.

10. Regular review: Periodically review the advice log to identify trends, assess the effectiveness of responses, and ensure that advice remains current and aligned with regulatory requirements.

By implementing these best practices, compliance managers can create a robust and useful advice log that enhances the quality and consistency of their advisory work.

Handling Complex Queries

To handle complex compliance queries effectively, and at the risk of repeating oneself, consider the following approach:

1. Implement a structured four-stage process:

- Gather comprehensive details about the query
- Ensure thorough understanding of all aspects
- Assess regulatory impacts of any decision
- Formulate and deliver the response, including any caveats or requirements

2. Utilise the "six honest serving-men" methodology to fully comprehend the query:

- What: Identify the exact nature of the query
- Why: Understand the reasons behind the query
- When: Determine relevant timelines and deadlines
- How: Consider the potential impact on the firm
- Who: Identify all stakeholders involved
- Where: Determine applicable jurisdictions and locations

3. Request written queries: Encourage colleagues to submit complex queries in writing, providing time for considered responses and maintaining an audit trail.

4. Consult widely: Don't hesitate to seek clarification or additional information from:

- The query originator
- Their manager or subordinates
- Other compliance department members
- Senior managers
- Industry association contacts
- Compliance colleagues in other firms

5. Conduct thorough research:

- Check all relevant definitions, glossaries, rules, and requirements
- Consider the situation from multiple perspectives
- Use reliable references such as the Oxford English Dictionary, internal policy documents, and regulatory handbooks

6. Take your time: Don't feel pressured to provide quick answers for complex queries. Ensure you fully understand the issue before responding.

7. Consider broader implications:

- Does the proposed action pass the "smell test"?
- Would you be comfortable seeing it reported in the Financial Times?
- How would you explain the decision to a regulator?
- If widely adopted, what impact would this practice have on the financial services industry?

8. Document your reasoning: Clearly explain the rationale behind your advice, citing relevant rules, regulations, and internal policies.

9. Follow up: After addressing the query, consider any necessary follow-up actions, such as:

- Reviewing or updating policies and procedures
- Identifying training needs
- Assessing potential regulatory notifications
- Evaluating governance implications

10. Maintain an advice log: Record all aspects of the query and your response, including:

- Enquiry method and person
- Specific area of concern
- Detailed query and response
- Relevant rules and regulations
- Time taken to address the query
- Any specific conditions
- Links to relevant correspondence

By following these steps, you can effectively handle complex compliance queries while ensuring thorough consideration of all relevant factors and maintaining a clear audit trail of your decision-making process.

Escalating a Compliance Query

Based on the information provided in the chapter, here are some effective ways to escalate a compliance query when you need further authority:

1. Follow the four-stage process:

- Obtain all relevant details about the query
- Ensure thorough understanding of the issue
- Determine the regulatory impacts of any decision
- Select your final response, including any requirements or caveats

2. Identify the need for escalation: If you've gone through the process and determined that you need additional authority or input, recognize this as part of your assessment.

3. Consult widely: Before escalating, consider consulting with:

- Other compliance department members
- Senior managers
- Industry association contacts
- Compliance colleagues in other firms

4. Document your reasoning: Clearly explain the rationale behind your need for escalation, citing relevant rules, regulations, and internal policies.

5. Prepare a comprehensive summary: Include all relevant information gathered using the "six honest serving-men" methodology (What, Why, When, How, Who, and Where).

6. Consider broader implications: Be prepared to discuss:

- How the issue passes (or fails) the "smell test"
- Potential media impact (e.g., Financial Times coverage)
- How you would explain the decision to a regulator
- The potential industry-wide impact if the practice were widely adopted

7. Identify the appropriate authority: Determine who has the necessary authority to make a decision on the issue, whether it's senior management, a specific committee, or even the board of directors.

8. Use your advice log: Reference any similar past queries and their resolutions to support your escalation.

9. Present options: If possible, provide multiple courses of action with their respective pros and cons, rather than just escalating the problem.

10. Highlight urgency and potential risks: Clearly communicate any time sensitivities and the potential consequences of delayed decision-making.

11. Propose a governance solution: If the issue is recurring, suggest forming a dedicated committee or forum to handle similar queries in the future.

12. Consider external escalation: If the issue cannot be resolved internally, be prepared to:

- Approach your trade body to gauge industry-wide sentiment
- Contact the regulator directly through their helpline
- Reserve the issue for inclusion in a future consultation paper response

By following these steps, you can effectively escalate complex compliance queries while ensuring that all relevant information is considered, and the appropriate authorities are involved in the decision-making process.

Summary

Compliance advisory work, while demanding and often time-consuming, plays a vital role in maintaining regulatory adherence and fostering a culture of compliance within an organisation. By employing structured approaches, maintaining comprehensive records, and considering the broader implications of each query, compliance professionals can provide invaluable guidance to their colleagues and stakeholders.

This work not only helps prevent regulatory breaches but also keeps compliance managers abreast of the latest developments and evolving trends in the financial services industry. Ultimately, effective compliance advisory work contributes significantly to the overall health and success of the organisation.

Chapter 14: Compliance with the FCA

We would all like to think that our firm is run not only compliantly but efficiently, like well-oiled machines. However, we understand that things can sometimes go awry. Being able to identify potential issues before they arise presents a significant opportunity to address situations proactively. In the words of Monty Python, "nobody expects the Spanish Inquisition," and similarly, many Compliance Managers and a firm's executives do not anticipate regulatory investigation.

Understanding the processes and possibilities of regulatory scrutiny is essential. When the worst happens, you will be required to explain processes, assess damage, and propose realistic outcomes for your company.

Familiarity with the route followed by regulators provides you with a workflow pathway, enabling prioritisation and appropriate sectoring of work should any rogue element within your firm presume to know better. While awareness of these procedures is a valuable tool, they should not be wielded as threats within the firm, as this will undermine your credibility.
The UK regulatory landscape features various regimes, yet the FCA (Financial Conduct Authority) predominates, particularly concerning conduct risk.

While those operating under dual regulation or in alternative jurisdictions must be cognisant of both the PRA (Prudential Regulation Authority) and FCA enforcement regimes, for most UK compliance practitioners, FCA rules prevail.

Monitoring, testing, remedying, and rectifying are vital functions under any regulator's purview. The enforcement department of the FCA is structured to:

- Deter poor conduct
- Provide clear corrective remedial action
- Penalise bad behaviour
- Offer a method of compensation to victims
- Promote high standards of competent behaviour

The FCA and PRA derive their powers from the Financial Services and Markets Act 2000 (FSMA), which provides broad disciplinary authority and the framework for both civil and criminal actions against firms or individuals, regardless of their FCA regulatory status. While the FCA does not make the rules—it follows procedural requirements alongside legislation such as the Proceeds of Crime Act and Human Rights Act 1998—its actions must be proportionate, fair, and transparent, as overseen by the Upper Tribunal.

Conduct Risk

"Conduct Risk" has become a ubiquitous term in financial services, yet many remain unclear about its precise implications. While a wealth of information (including failure reasons and fines) points to the right direction, a search for "Conduct Risk" in the FCA's handbook yields little, indicating no specific definition in the glossary.

From our experience designing and implementing conduct risk frameworks, several focus areas emerge, including:

- Aligning business models with fair treatment of customers
- Complaints handling
- Product development and governance
- Product Intervention
- Remuneration and reward policies
- Financial promotion withdrawal and prohibition
- Conflicts of interest
- Incentives
- Wholesale
- Business continuity

Conduct risk derives not just from past mis-selling scandals but is embedded in the Treating Customers Fairly (TCF) initiatives and Conduct of Business Sourcebook (COBS) rules.

The ambiguity of the term's definition allows firms to interpret and apply it subjectively. The Retail Distribution Review (RDR), effective from 31 December 2012, significantly altered investment advice market business models, compounded by the implementation of MiFID II (Markets in Financial Instruments Directive) and an FCA with a more intrusive supervisory stance. Many firms lack awareness of the elements at play and risk exposure during assessments or regulatory visits.

The importance of Conduct Risk is not limited to the UK but extends globally, affecting many international regulators.

Understanding and Demonstrating "Conduct Risk"

To effectively manage conduct risk, you must first grasp where it sits within your organisation. Citing the FCA Risk Outlook from 2013 onwards, determine potential risk areas. Most of these fall under Operational Risk, a field where some consultancies can offer assistance. You don't necessarily need costly software for many mid-sized firms, but you must understand how to identify risks and take corrective action. According to SYSC (Senior Management Arrangements, Systems and Controls) 7.1.2 R of the FCA Handbook, a "*common platform firm must establish, implement, and maintain adequate risk management policies and procedures, including effective procedures for risk assessment.*"

Operational Risk is often defined by Basel II as "the risk of loss resulting from inadequate or failed internal processes, people, systems, or external events." Identifying these risks is just the beginning; measuring and addressing them poses a real challenge and often requires significant work from firms not typically engaged in this area.
A Conduct Risk Framework helps in identifying elements impacted. Through this, proportionate measurements for reporting can be devised. Combined with a rational appetite for risk, this data offers an exceptional reporting level for Senior Management to consider.

Management's three phases—definition and measurement, management, and activity execution—parallel business operations. Effective management results from activity's by-product; hence, no definitive management method exists. Accurate data provision between phases is key. Unfortunately, management information is frequently defined incorrectly, undermining efforts.

The FCA's General Enforcement Powers

Under FSMA, the FCA has extensive disciplinary, criminal, and civil powers to act against regulated and non-regulated entities not meeting required standards. Examples include:

- Withdrawal of a firm's authorisation
- Prohibition of individuals in financial services
- Prevention of specific regulated activities by individuals
- Firm suspensions up to 12 months from regulated activities
- Individual suspensions up to 2 years from controlled functions

- Publicly censuring firms and individuals
- Imposition of financial penalties
- Seeking injunctions or asset freezing orders
- Application for restitution orders
- Prosecution of unauthorised regulated activities

While this may be engaging reading, we'll focus on:

- Identifying regulatory discovery methods
- Highlighting regulator's hot buttons
- Understanding scrutiny methods
- Outlining recourse options in regulatory scrutiny
- Exploring potential outcomes for misconduct

Chapter 15 will address compliance risk assessment, while Chapter 16 will prepare you for regulatory visits.

Information, Information, Information

The FCA mandates numerous reporting requirements and has access to many public records, including HMRC filings and Companies House reports. With this information, the FCA builds a risk profile of your firm concerning its statutory objectives. Social media monitoring increasingly aids regulatory and law enforcement monitoring of illegal promotions or misleading statements.

Several regular reporting and notification requirements facilitate the FCA's monitoring efforts, typically involving:

- Auditors' reports: Regulated firms must appoint auditors with access to records. It's a criminal offence under section 346 of FSMA to mislead an auditor. Auditors must provide the FCA with reports on regulatory activities, comment on internal controls, and submit client asset reports where applicable.
- Variation of Permissions (VOP) requests: Application for VOP might trigger scrutiny if suspicion arises that you are acting without requisite permissions.
- Rule waiver requests: Requesting a waiver or rule modification might flag concerns requiring FCA inquiry.
- Direct FCA consultations: While engaging with the FCA on issues is essential, recognise it may lead to further inquiry.
- ONA Report: Information from the forms regarding approved persons or instances of dismissal may instigate an FCA review.
- Regulatory reporting: Includes capital adequacy, appointed reps/approved persons, and overseas regulators linked to the firm.
- Controller or close link reporting: If linked to dubious firms, the FCA may inquire about such involvements.

Beyond periodic reporting, the FCA can conduct monitoring visits, whether planned or impromptu. Such monitoring extends contractually to firm suppliers or outsourcers.

Mystery Shopping

To evaluate advice standards, suitability, and recommendation processes, the FCA might conduct undisclosed visits or calls to your firm. Retail firms, in particular, are frequent targets of such assessments.

Other Regulatory Bodies

The FCA collaborates with other regulators, both within the EU and globally. International scrutiny on your firm due to external jurisdiction concerns could lead to intensified investigation.

The FCA also identifies firm activities via media channels, complaints, or promotions flagged by the Advertising Standards Authority (ASA). Whistleblowing under the Public Interest Disclosure Act 1998 (PIDA) can also prompt FCA investigation. Engaging with the FCA truthfully and openly, as mandated by Principle 11, is paramount during any investigation. Attempts to obscure facts or deceive only serve to antagonise regulators further. If an error or unintentional rule breach occurs, transparency is the best approach, maintaining regulatory integrity.

Professional Assistance

Engaging professional services, including legal, accounting, and compliance consultant firms, can provide much-needed guidance and expertise in navigating FCA enforcement processes.

Personal Representation and FSMT

The Financial Services and Markets Tribunal (FSMT) is an independent adjudicative body in the United Kingdom that handles appeals related to decisions made by various financial services regulators, including the Financial Conduct Authority (FCA) and the Prudential Regulation Authority (PRA). Here's an overview of its key functions:

Purpose and Functions:

1. **Appeals Process**: The FSMT provides a forum for individuals and organisations to appeal against decisions made by financial regulators. This includes decisions around penalties, licensing, and regulatory approvals.
2. **Independent Adjudication**: It ensures that appeals are conducted fairly and independently, allowing for a thorough examination of the evidence and legal arguments presented by both sides.
3. **Legal and Regulatory Expertise**: The tribunal consists of legally trained members as well as experts in financial services, ensuring that decisions are made based on a solid understanding of both legal and financial principles.
4. **Judicial Review**: The FSMT can review decisions made by regulatory bodies to ensure they comply with the law and follow proper procedures. This includes checking if decisions were made in a reasonable manner and based on relevant evidence.

5. **Public Interest**: The tribunal plays a role in upholding the principles of transparency and accountability in the financial services sector, which is vital for maintaining public confidence in the financial system.

Composition:

- The FSMT is typically composed of judges from the Upper Tribunal, alongside representatives with expertise in finance. This combination ensures that both legal and sector-specific insights are applied in decision-making.

Procedures:

- The tribunal follows a structured process for hearing cases, which includes the submission of evidence, written arguments, and oral hearings. Parties involved in an appeal can present their case and challenge the decisions of the financial regulators.

Significance:

- The FSMT is crucial for ensuring that regulatory decisions are fair and proportionate, providing a necessary check on the powers of financial regulators and allowing for recourse when individuals or organisations feel they have been treated unjustly.

Related Topics:

- Financial regulation, consumer protection, enforcement actions, and regulatory compliance are all relevant areas associated with the work of the FSMT.

Essentially, the Tribunal can:

- Uphold FCA decisions
- Prevent or modify FCA action
- Recommend rule/procedure adjustments

Media Relations

In extreme dissatisfaction with FCA treatment, you might consider engaging the press, though this should be a last resort due to media unpredictability in defining public interest.

Publicity and Enforcement

While the FCA generally refrains from commenting on investigations, they may publish appropriate information pertaining to serious cases upon issuing Decision or Final Notices. The FCA employs mediation processes, where mutually acceptable solutions are sought out, though such options are less likely in criminal or urgent cases.

Trade Associations and Legal Advice

Contacting trade associations may provide case support, particularly if broader membership implications exist. Legal advice is strongly recommended for understanding additional recourse.

Potential Outcomes and Settlements

Various FCA actions may ensue from disciplinary investigations, as detailed in their Decision Procedure and Penalties Manual (DEPP).

Settlements, possible at any stage, are negotiated with FCA Directors or Department Heads.

While settlement discussions are held without prejudice, unresolved cases revert to the Regulatory Decisions Committee (RDC), independent of admissions or concessions during settlement talks. Settlements reflect FCA, statutory, and operational objectives with penalty discounts available at various stages:

- Stage 1 (early): 30%
- Stage 2 (prior to RDC written representations): 20%
- Stage 3 (before Decision Notice): 10%

While DEPP outlines potential FCA actions, other outcomes exist beyond non-action. Potential options include:

- Informal requests to update the FCA
- Individual guidance clarifications
- FCA-initiated permission variances
- Permission withdrawals
- Injunctions or asset freezes
- Withdrawal of approved person status
- Individual prohibitions
- Redress and compensation
- Insolvency orders
- Public censures
- Fines and prosecutions
- Private warnings

- Notifications/assistance from other authorities
- Non-FCA action
- Damage to reputation or contracts
- Firm closures

Reviewing the FCA's website for final notices reveals ongoing enforcement actions, emphasising compliance importance. Avoid ignoring rules that could imperil your firm. The FCA Enforcement Information Guide details enforcement powers comprehensively.

Conclusion:

The Financial Services and Markets Tribunal serves a vital role in the UK's financial regulatory framework, promoting fairness and accountability, thereby fostering a stable and trustworthy financial services sector.

Chapter 15: Compliance Risk Assessment

Compliance Risk Assessment

In the ever-evolving landscape of financial services regulation, the importance of a robust compliance risk assessment cannot be overstated. This critical process enables firms to identify, evaluate, and mitigate potential risks associated with regulatory compliance. By conducting thorough assessments, organisations can proactively address vulnerabilities, allocate resources effectively, and maintain a strong compliance posture.

Understanding Compliance Risk

Compliance risk refers to the potential for legal or regulatory sanctions, financial loss, or reputational damage resulting from an organisation's failure to comply with applicable laws, regulations, codes of conduct, or standards of good practice. In the UK financial services sector, compliance risk is particularly significant due to the complex and dynamic regulatory environment overseen by bodies such as the Financial Conduct Authority (FCA) and the Prudential Regulation Authority (PRA).

The Importance of Compliance Risk Assessment

A well-executed compliance risk assessment serves several crucial purposes:

1. **Identification of Vulnerabilities**: It helps firms pinpoint areas where they may be exposed to compliance breaches.

2. **Resource Allocation**: By highlighting high-risk areas, it allows for more efficient allocation of compliance resources.

3. **Regulatory Preparedness**: It aids in preparing for regulatory inspections and demonstrates a proactive approach to compliance.

4. **Risk Mitigation**: It enables the development of targeted strategies to mitigate identified risks.

5. **Cultural Enhancement**: It fosters a culture of compliance throughout the organisation.

Key Components of a Compliance Risk Assessment

1. Regulatory Landscape Analysis

Begin by conducting a comprehensive review of the current regulatory environment. This should include:

- Identifying all relevant laws, regulations, and industry standards applicable to your firm.

- Reviewing recent regulatory changes and upcoming legislation that may impact your business.
- Analysing enforcement actions and fines in your sector to understand regulatory focus areas.

2. Business Model Evaluation

Assess how your firm's business model interacts with regulatory requirements:

- Review your products, services, and target markets.
- Identify high-risk activities or areas prone to compliance issues.
- Consider any planned changes to your business model that may introduce new compliance risks.

3. Internal Control Environment

Evaluate the effectiveness of your existing compliance framework:

- Review policies, procedures, and controls designed to ensure regulatory compliance.
- Assess the roles and responsibilities of compliance staff and other key personnel.
- Examine the effectiveness of your compliance monitoring and reporting processes.

4. Risk Identification and Assessment

Systematically identify and assess compliance risks:

- Conduct workshops or interviews with key stakeholders across the business.
- Use risk assessment tools such as risk matrices to evaluate the likelihood and impact of potential compliance breaches.
- Consider both inherent risks (before controls) and residual risks (after controls).

5. Gap Analysis

Compare your current compliance practices against regulatory requirements and industry best practices:

- Identify areas where your firm may fall short of regulatory expectations.
- Assess the adequacy of your compliance resources and expertise.
- Evaluate the effectiveness of your compliance training programmes.

6. Technology and Data Management

Assess the role of technology in your compliance efforts:

- Review the systems used for compliance monitoring and reporting.
- Evaluate data management practices, including data protection and privacy measures.
- Consider the potential for technology-enabled compliance solutions, such as RegTech tools.

7. Third-Party Risk

Evaluate compliance risks associated with third-party relationships:

- Assess the compliance practices of key vendors, partners, and outsourced service providers.
- Review contracts and service level agreements for compliance-related clauses.
- Consider the potential impact of third-party actions on your firm's compliance status.

Conducting the Assessment

When carrying out a compliance risk assessment, consider the following approach:

1. **Planning**: Define the scope, objectives, and methodology of the assessment. Identify key stakeholders and resources required.

2. **Data Gathering**: Collect relevant information through document reviews, interviews, surveys, and system analyses.

3. **Risk Analysis**: Evaluate the collected data to identify and prioritise compliance risks. Use quantitative and qualitative methods as appropriate.

4. **Reporting**: Document the findings, including identified risks, their potential impact, and recommended mitigation strategies.

5. **Action Planning**: Develop a detailed plan to address identified risks, including timelines, responsibilities, and resource requirements.

6. **Monitoring and Review**: Implement ongoing monitoring of the action plan and regularly review the effectiveness of risk mitigation measures.

Best Practices for Compliance Risk Assessment

To enhance the effectiveness of your compliance risk assessment, consider the following best practices:

- Senior Management Involvement: Ensure that senior management is actively engaged in the risk assessment process and supports its outcomes.

- Cross-Functional Approach: Involve representatives from various departments to gain a holistic view of compliance risks across the organisation.

- Regular Updates: Conduct risk assessments at least annually, with more frequent reviews in rapidly changing regulatory environments.

- Documentation: Maintain detailed records of the assessment process, findings, and subsequent actions to demonstrate due diligence to regulators.

- Continuous Improvement: Use the insights gained from each assessment to refine and improve your compliance programme over time.

- External Perspective: Consider engaging external compliance consultants to provide an objective view and industry benchmarking.

Emerging Trends in Compliance Risk Assessment

As the regulatory landscape continues to evolve, several trends are shaping the future of compliance risk assessment:

- **Data Analytics**: Advanced analytics and artificial intelligence are increasingly being used to identify patterns and predict potential compliance issues.

- **Integrated Risk Management**: Firms are moving towards a more holistic approach, integrating compliance risk assessment with other risk management processes.

- **Real-Time Monitoring**: Continuous monitoring tools are enabling firms to identify and respond to compliance risks more quickly.

- **Culture and Conduct**: There is a growing focus on assessing the cultural aspects of compliance, including employee behaviour and decision-making processes.

- Environmental, Social, and Governance (ESG) Considerations: Regulatory attention on ESG issues is increasing, necessitating their inclusion in compliance risk assessments.

Common Compliance Risks

The most common compliance risks facing UK financial services firms in recent years include:

1. **Financial crime and anti-money laundering (AML) failures** - This was cited as a major area where firms faced penalties and enforcement action from regulators.

2. **Systems and controls issues** - Inadequate compliance systems, processes and controls were frequently highlighted as problems.

3. **Governance and oversight failings** - Poor governance structures and lack of proper oversight were common issues.

4. **Market abuse surveillance** - Failures in systems and processes to detect and prevent market abuse.

5. **Regulatory reporting failures** - Issues with accurate and timely regulatory reporting.

6. **Consumer protection/conduct risk** - Failures in treating customers fairly and providing suitable advice/products.

7. **Cybersecurity and data protection** - Growing risks around cyber attacks and data breaches.

8. **ESG compliance** - Increasing regulatory focus on environmental, social and governance issues.

9. **Keeping up with regulatory changes** - Firms struggling to stay on top of evolving regulations.

10. **Record keeping deficiencies** - Poor documentation and record keeping practices.

11. **Use of unauthorised communication channels** - Issues around staff using personal devices/apps.

12. **Outsourcing and third-party risk management** - Managing risks from outsourced functions and third parties.

13. **Financial promotions and marketing materials** - Ensuring compliant marketing and communications.

The research indicates many firms are struggling with the increasing regulatory burden and complexity of compliance requirements. Key challenges include manual processes, lack of resources, and difficulty keeping pace with regulatory changes. Investing in technology, automation and staff training were cited as important ways firms are trying to address these compliance risks.

Risk Rating Guidance:

Risk rating these areas will help you form a potential identifier for where you may need to concentrate your efforts in risk mitigation. The Financial Ombudsman Service (FOS) Report is a good indicator of things that people complain about. Check it out and relate it to your business, products or services.

Although this is provided as guidance you could define further levels and it is often useful to attach a monetary or number of customers value to them (as appropriate) so that you can start to form a risk appetite. Risk elements to consider are;

- **Low** –
  - None or minor penalties or consequences;
  - Not a current regulatory priority;
  - Noncomplex requirement
  - Not an area that we generally have issues with

- **Medium** –
  - Potential for moderate penalties and/or consequences;
  - Currently a moderate focus or priority for regulators
  - Moderately complex with incomplete regulatory guidance
  - Periodic errors noted by examiners and testers

- **High** –
    - Potential for significant penalties and/or consequences
    - Currently a high priority of regulators
    - Highly complex requirement with incomplete regulatory guidance
    - One of the leading areas where errors are noted

Reputation Risk Considerations

What is the level of public and customer concern/publicity over noncompliance?

- Low – No or low concern likely;
- Medium – Moderate concern possible;
- High – Significant concern or loss of customer confidence likely

Operational Risk Considerations

Although this can often be subjective, we have found it best carried out with at least two people, preferably as a workshop. These are only guidelines and can be amended by you as required.

Simply evaluate the risk associated with the presence or absence of internal controls, processes, and procedures to maintain compliance; the degree of centralisation or decentralisation; level of automation to eliminate human error; staff turnover that could contribute to errors; and existence of adequate training, annual testing or other competence measures.

- **Low** –
    - Presence of good internal controls, processes, and procedures to maintain compliance
    - Centralised
    - Partially or fully automated
    - Low staff turnover
    - Adequate training has been provided
    - Account opened Face-to-Face on site (no distance sales)
- Customer is local, (lives/works)

- **Medium** –
    - Some weaknesses or soft areas in internal controls, processes, or procedures
    - Partially decentralised
    - Some automation
    - Moderate staff turnover
    - Minimal training provided infrequently

  - Account opened Face-to-Face off site (no distance sales)

- ➢ Customer located relatively local (within 100 miles) and is maintained adequately

- **High** –

  - Weak or no internal controls, processes or procedures
  - Decentralised
  - Not automated
  - High staff turnover
  - No training provided
  - Account not opened Face-to-Face

- ➢ Customer located over 100 miles away and much business is done by phone/online videocalls/email.

Probability of Error Risk Considerations

Evaluate the risk that error will occur due to prior history of error and changes in regulatory requirements, products, and/or services.

Test/Audit/Exam Results

  - Low – No errors in last review;
  - Moderate – Minor errors in last review;
  - High – Significant errors in last review

Change in regulatory requirements

- Low – No changes since last monitored;
- Moderate – Minor changes since last monitored;
- High – Significant changes since last monitored

Change in product / service

- Low – No changes since last monitored;
- Moderate – Minor changes since last monitored;
- High – Significant changes since last monitored

--- End of Guidance Notes ---

Methodology

Phase 1 – Data Collection

Step One: Products and Services

Compile an exhaustive list of the products and services your firm offers. Consider all areas of operation, from investment and insurance to support services like tax planning and debt counselling. This inventory forms the basis for mapping regulatory obligations.

Step Two: Systems and Controls

Identify existing controls through departmental interviews, focusing on policies, procedures, and automation levels.

Evaluate the centralisation of processes, training adequacy, staff turnover, and IT management plans. This assessment ensures a comprehensive understanding of your controls and potential gaps.

Step Three: Applicable Regulations

Chart the primary regulatory requirements applicable to your listed products and services. This regulatory map should encompass not just FCA rules but also other relevant legislative instruments, including data protection and employment laws, ensuring a holistic view of compliance obligations.

Phase 2 – Inherent Risk Analysis

Step One: Regulatory Risk

Understand the FCA's current regulatory focus areas. These "hot buttons" may include issues like collective investment schemes or structured product mis-selling. Risk-rating these areas helps prioritise efforts in compliance and risk mitigation.

Step Two: Reputation Risk

Evaluate the public and customer perceptions of compliance risk. The level of concern or potential loss of confidence can vary significantly and influence overall risk management strategies.

Step Three: Inherent Risk

Assess the inherent risk for each product and service, considering both regulatory and reputation risks without the influence of existing controls. This provides a baseline risk profile that informs subsequent assessments and mitigations.

Phase 3 – Residual Risk Analysis

Step One: Operational Risk

Evaluate the impact of operational controls on risk management. Consider factors such as control robustness, process automation, staff turnover, and the training provided. Residual operational risk reflects the effectiveness of these measures post-control implementation.

Step Two: Probability of Error Risk

Assess the likelihood of errors based on past performance, regulatory changes, and product/service evolution. This analysis helps identify areas where error risks are significant and direct focus towards those needing further control enhancements.

Step Three: Residual Risk

Determine the residual risk by analysing operational and probability of error risks, providing a refined risk profile post-control application. This analysis drives targeted risk management strategies.

Phase 4 – Overall Risk Analysis and Follow-up

Step One: Overall Risk

Develop a visual representation of risk levels across products and services. Colour-coded charts facilitate quick assessments by stakeholders and aid in communication with management and regulators.

Step Two: Management Tolerance of Compliance Risk

Define management's risk appetite. Document any acceptable high-risk areas and ensure rigorous monitoring of controls where risk tolerance is low. Tailor strategies to align with management's overall compliance philosophy.

Step Three: Direction of Risk

Forecast risk direction and trends for the coming year. Anticipating these changes ensures proactive risk management and promotes adaptive strategies in a dynamic regulatory environment.

By adhering to these processes and maintaining an open dialogue with regulatory updates, firms can ensure they manage compliance risks effectively, supporting long-term stability and regulatory adherence.

Mitigating Compliance Risks

Ways firms can effectively mitigate compliance risks:

1. Conduct regular compliance risk assessments:

- Systematically identify, evaluate and prioritise legal and regulatory compliance risks
- Review at least annually or when there are changes in the business or regulatory environment
- Use assessments to allocate resources to the most critical risks

2. Develop robust compliance policies and procedures:

- Create clear guidelines and expected behaviours for employees
- Ensure policies align with industry best practices and regulations
- Review and update policies regularly

3. Implement strong internal controls and monitoring:

- Design systems and controls to mitigate identified risks
- Conduct ongoing monitoring of compliance processes
- Periodically test effectiveness of controls

4. Provide comprehensive staff training:

- Train employees on compliance requirements and procedures
- Ensure staff understand their compliance responsibilities
- Offer regular refresher training as regulations change

5. Adopt a risk-based approach:

- Focus resources on highest risk areas
- Tailor compliance efforts to specific risks faced by the business
- Prioritise mitigation of most significant risks

6. Leverage compliance technology:

- Use GRC tools to manage compliance processes
- Automate monitoring and reporting where possible

- Implement systems for tracking regulatory changes

7. Conduct third-party due diligence:

- Assess compliance risks of vendors and partners
- Ensure third parties meet regulatory requirements
- Monitor ongoing compliance of third parties

8. Foster a culture of compliance:

- Set the right "tone from the top" on compliance importance
- Integrate compliance into business processes and decision-making
- Encourage reporting of compliance issues

9. Stay current on regulatory changes:

- Monitor for new and changing regulations
- Assess impact of regulatory changes on the business
- Update compliance program as needed

10. Consider external expertise:

- Engage compliance consultants for specialized knowledge
- Get external perspective on compliance program effectiveness
- Use external audits to identify gaps

The key is taking a proactive, risk-based approach to compliance and integrating it throughout the organisation's operations and culture. Regular assessment, strong policies/controls, staff training, and leveraging technology are all critical components of an effective compliance risk mitigation program.

Conclusion

A thorough and well-executed compliance risk assessment is a cornerstone of effective regulatory compliance. By systematically identifying, evaluating, and addressing compliance risks, firms can not only avoid regulatory sanctions but also enhance their operational efficiency and reputation. In an era of increasing regulatory scrutiny and rapid technological change, a proactive approach to compliance risk management is more critical than ever.

Remember, compliance risk assessment is not a one-time exercise but an ongoing process that should evolve with your business and the regulatory environment. By embedding this process into your organisation's DNA, you can create a resilient compliance framework that supports sustainable growth and maintains the trust of regulators, customers, and stakeholders alike.

Chapter 16: Preparing for a Regulatory Visit

When you know a visit from a regulatory body is on the horizon, particularly if it is the Financial Conduct Authority (FCA) in the UK, it becomes extremely important to fully understand what this regulator expects from you and how they operate. With the recent changes in regulatory practices, businesses now must adapt and respond swiftly in order to stay in compliance and ensure they are always ready.

Evolving Regulatory Processes

The Financial Conduct Authority has moved away from the previous regulator's model, known as the 'Advanced Risk Responsive Operating FrameWork' (ARROW), which was first developed by the Financial Services Authority (FSA). They now embrace more flexible inspection strategies, including thematic reviews and targeted evaluations known as "Deep Dives." These new strategies enable the regulator to dive more deeply into specific areas within a firm's operations. They focus especially on risks related to conduct and the protection of consumers. This change signals a shift toward a more interventionist and proactive form of supervision. There is a strong emphasis on making sure firms are following best practices in managing risk and governance.

Understanding FCA's Authority and Enforcement Options

Under the Financial Services and Markets Act 2000 (FSMA), the FCA has extensive powers to take various actions to make sure firms meet their obligations under the regulations. These powers are broad and include the ability to withdraw firm authorisations, impose individual prohibitions, suspend firms from conducting regulated activities, levy financial penalties, and even freeze assets. To ensure thorough oversight, the FCA collaborates closely with other law enforcement agencies.

Section 166 Reports

A key tool that the FCA frequently uses is the Section 166 report, which is also known as a Skilled Person's Review. These reports allow the FCA to thoroughly investigate a firm's operations or aspects related to financial prudence. Recent data from the FCA highlights that the issuance of these reports has remained consistent over time. This consistency underscores their importance as a standard tool for detailed analysis without immediately moving to more severe enforcement measures. More information is below.

Regulatory Focus and Preparation for Visits

The FCA's areas of focus can often be identified from their Annual Plan and other published materials. These documents outline current priorities like cybersecurity, preventing financial crime, and ensuring consumer protection. It is essential for firms to prepare for potential oversight by making sure their compliance systems are strong and thoroughly documented.

This preparation should involve regular internal reviews and proactively addressing any weak areas. Seeking help from external compliance consultants might be necessary to ensure complete readiness.

Early and Thorough Planning

As soon as you receive notice of an FCA visit, if not earlier, preparation should begin immediately. Important steps in this preparation include assembling a cross-departmental team led by senior management. Ensuring that there is buy-in from all organisational levels and appointing experienced staff to communicate with the FCA during the visit are critical. It is also crucial to keep open lines of communication and to have clarity regarding the visit's objectives and the FCA's particular areas of interest.

Document Preparation and Staff Communication

You will need to prepare comprehensive, up-to-date documentation, which should include governance frameworks, organisational charts, minutes from relevant meetings, compliance monitoring records, and risk management documentation. Informing staff throughout the organisation about the importance of the FCA review and their specific roles is vital. Training team members on how to respond to requests for information and how to conduct themselves during interviews can help reduce stress and ensure effective communication with the regulator.

Handling Interviews and Submission Accuracy

During the FCA visit, it is important for those being interviewed to be well-prepared and to respond to questions with precision, sharing only information that falls within their knowledge.

Interviews are not intended to test memory; therefore, providing relevant documents to support answers is recommended. Having a member of the compliance team present during interviews is beneficial for ensuring accurate communication and providing immediate answers to queries.

The FCA aims to understand not just whether firms are following procedures but also how effectively they cultivate a culture of risk awareness and governance that meets industry standards. Consequently, it is important for executives to clearly explain how their strategic objectives align with risk management frameworks and to show evidence of how these elements are fully integrated into their business practices.

Post-Visit Actions and Continuous Improvement

After a regulatory visit concludes, firms should carefully review the feedback provided by the FCA and create a clear plan of action to address any weaknesses identified. Keeping detailed records of all remediation efforts is crucial. Providing regular progress reports can ensure transparency with the regulator. Organisations can benefit from conducting workshops or reviews to reflect on the process, thereby internalizing the lessons learned and improving future regulatory interactions.

Effective Preparation

To prepare effectively for regulatory scrutiny, firms should concentrate on strong risk management, transparent governance, and proactive compliance practices.

Engaging early with regulatory consultants, conducting in-depth internal evaluations, and fostering a culture of compliance can help reduce risks and establish a foundation for a positive relationship with regulators. Focusing on these key elements will not only help firms meet regulatory requirements but also enhance their overall efficiency and the confidence of their stakeholders.

The FCA holds a broad array of powers concerning authorised firms, which are granted under the Financial Services and Markets Act 2000 (FSMA). These powers enable the FCA to ensure that firms comply with regulatory obligations and protect consumers. Here are some of the key powers:

1. **Authorisation and Supervision**: The FCA authorises firms to carry out regulated activities in the UK. It monitors these firms on an ongoing basis to ensure they adhere to required standards and can withdraw authorisation if firms fail to comply.
2. **Enforcement Actions**: The FCA can take enforcement actions against firms and individuals who violate regulatory requirements. Such actions can include issuing financial penalties, public censure, and taking criminal proceedings for serious breaches.

3. **Variation and Cancellation of Permission**: The FCA has the power to vary the permissions it grants to firms, restricting the activities they can undertake. It can also cancel the permissions entirely, effectively shutting down a firm's regulated activities.
4. **Imposing Requirements**: The FCA can impose specific requirements on a firm, such as the need to maintain higher levels of capital or liquidity, or to make changes to their management or systems and controls, to prevent potential consumer harm or to address specific risks identified by the FCA.
5. **Prohibition Orders**: The FCA can issue prohibition orders which prevent individuals from carrying out specific regulated activities if they are deemed not to be fit and proper persons.
6. **Skilled Person Reviews (Section 166)**: The FCA can mandate a firm to commission a report from a "skilled person" to investigate and report on certain areas of concern. This helps the FCA to assess compliance with regulatory requirements or address complex issues within a firm.
7. **Asset Freezes and Injunctions**: In cases where there is a significant risk to consumers or the market, the FCA can apply for court orders to freeze assets and obtain injunctions to prevent particular actions by firms or individuals.
8. **Redress and Restitution Orders**: The FCA can require firms to compensate customers who have suffered losses due to regulatory breaches or misconduct.

9. **Marketplace Oversight**: Beyond regulating individual firms, the FCA also oversees the functioning of financial markets, ensuring they operate efficiently and transparently. This includes regulating market infrastructures such as exchanges and clearinghouses.

These powers enable the FCA to protect consumers, maintain market integrity, and promote effective competition in financial markets. The FCA works towards ensuring that financial services operate fairly and efficiently, thus upholding the interests of consumers and the overall economy.

The Visit Starting Point

Firms and individuals are rightly concerned that as a result of reviews increasing in their intensity the FCA themselves are much better prepared and more skilled in a wider range of business models and categories now, resulting in a much more robust challenge with increased emphasis on risk rating and benchmarking.

The FCA itself is showing that it is preparing more thoroughly for acting fast where enforcement action may be required. The FCA has included technical specialists as members of their visit team and appears to be viewing firms as part of an overall sector and systemic themed approach, rather than the previously more individualised stance. This has been further demonstrated by half of firms experiencing an increase in the number of pre-visit documents requested, and the documentation sent was seen to have been considered thoroughly by the FCA.

A themed visit is not designed to catch you out or to tell you how to run your business specifically, and it is possible for firms to avoid sustaining any 'injury' or unwelcome outcome from an FCA review. Firms and individuals can be proactive and take action to prepare not only for the review process but to embed a culture within the firm that encompasses best practice, compliant behaviours and risk awareness.

The regulatory themed review involves anything from, an online questionnaire, a telephone or face to face interview or an on-site inspection visit focusing on a firm's systems and controls, entire risk management and governance. The Risk assessment considers the impact and probability of failure. The impact assessment is determined by the size of the firm and its sector, and the probability assessment determines the approach to the type of supervision a firm can expect going forward.

Early Planning for any assessment

Like the famous Boy Scouts Motto, the key to any regulatory visit, and particularly a regulatory review; even if remotely conducted, you should "Be prepared" and be prepared as early as you can, being proactive as soon as you can. Awaiting the receipt of the initial notification can often be too late.

It's always best to engage your Compliance Consultant as early on as possible if you are not used to this type of intervention as they know what to expect and the best ways to position the firm to the regulator.

Typically, firms will receive ample notice of a routine regulatory visit, but this can be severely cut short if the visit is part of an investigation. If the latter is the case, although not in all cases, the chances are you have probably been involved in the lead up to the investigation anyhow.

- The notice should clearly state or, you should try to clarify;
- The reason for the visit;
- The matters to be reviewed (themed visit or Deep Dive?);
- The documents and records to be reviewed (documentation request and for on-site visit);
- The category and number of people to be interviewed;
- The number and function of the regulators staff and their roles.

There are times when the timing of the visit is just not practical due to key staff absence due to holidays or sabbaticals, maternity leave etc., inspection by another regulatory body or locally holiday "shutdowns" (less likely these days, but still a consideration) mean that administrative staff may well be thin on the ground.

The first step is to appoint a project sponsor, and this will usually be the person responsible for Compliance. It is critical that your senior management buy in to this process not only making it a high priority but also aligning and committing resources.

Secondly, appoint a cross-function Project team (or maybe just one person) who is likely to be an office manager or someone who knows the administration system, the advisers, governance procedures and even elements of the risk practices. Your Firm should be able to demonstrate good corporate governance and that their risk management processes and practices are embedded throughout the organisation. The aim is for Firms to demonstrate that the key risks faced by the Firm as a whole and by each part of the Firm are identified, understood and recorded and that mitigating controls are in place. Although senior management responsibility has been a long-held tenet of the FCA, there is an increasing focus by FCA to hold individuals to account. We provide a separate Compliance Risk Assessment Guide free on request.

Thirdly, your entire staff will need to know what an FCA Review is, what it means to the firm and how they are to respond. People are normally protective of their family and their working environment and may well be tempted to put up a false front with anything they think is not important: this needs to be explained to them in detail, perhaps over a series of briefings, more frequently as the visit date approaches.

Point to note here is that if you have any outsourced functions at all, the proper documentation and requirements are in place as per FCA Handbook Senior Management Arrangements, Systems and Controls (SYSC) Chapter 8.

Business process documentation should be complete and up-to-date. An important part of the review preparation, to be undertaken several months in advance, is to identify where there may be deficiencies and 'getting the house in order' with respect to business controls, audit and record keeping. Prior to receiving the interview or information request it is useful to think about the information that may be requested.

Typically this will include Board and Committee Minutes for the previous 12 months; Organisation Chart; Management Information Packs for at least 6 or even 12 months; Business Plans including strategy and financial plans for at least this year but typically next 2-3; Business Continuity Plans, not just where you store the computer records; Compliance Monitoring Programmes and internal audit reports up to perhaps the last three years, Complaints records, Risk Register, ICAP/ICAS, RMARs and other regulatory submissions.
However, the information requests can also include details of Board attendance, details on outsourcing agreements and, increasingly, information on product lifecycle.

Firms should have conducted an assessment of the strengths and weaknesses of their own risk capabilities and show how these have been addressed prior to the review. There should be no surprises.

Don't be in a rush to send the documentation off as soon as part of it is obtained. Before you respond you should ensure that the documentation is carefully prepared, clear and complete, labelled clearly and even with separators to make sure nothing is mixed up with other documents.

Information should be accurate, current and appropriately signed off according to your matrix of authority or other documented internal process. This part of the process is critical to creating the best impression. You should use a third party (external Compliance Consultancy) to critically review the information – are there gaps/weaknesses, what further questions does it raise, does it demonstrate sound governance and effective risk management practices, or does it appear like a mish-mash of things thrown together?

All of these elements have to be robust, cohesive and congruent with your firm's practice. Any attempt at manufacturing, amending or otherwise "tidying" up will be spotted a mile off.

Make sure you ask the right questions. Is there an appropriate quantity and quality of management information and evidence of effective decision making and monitoring? Are the right judgements being made? Are the decisions fully documented and annotated accordingly? Have policies been reviewed recently, amended and is there evidence of their approval? Is version control used for all documentation, including customer facing documents?

Points to note, which may cause anxiety are; any areas where the firm is unclear as to exactly what the FCA requires should be followed up as soon as possible. A copy (or ensure easy reproduction) should be maintained of all submissions to the FCA, together with all other recent submissions, e.g., RMAR and transaction reporting data. All your senior managers should be made aware of the information requested by and submitted to the FCA. You should also be aware that any documentation requested is likely to form the basis of at least some interview questions. Nearer to the time of the visit the interviewees themselves should understand and be familiar with the information which has been provided.

Some coaching in formal interviews may also be needed for individuals and it may be worth considering hiring an HR professional or trainer to conduct sessions at your offices. All interviewees should be aware of relevant evidence and examples to demonstrate how governance and risk management works in the organisation and to show how significant decisions have been made, relevant to their role.

The FCA focus will be obviously specific to the Firm, the sector and generic "hot topics". A part of the pre-visit planning will be to identify what areas the FCA will focus on and anticipate the questions they may ask. Don't forget the FCA are practiced at using questions and use a three-level approach generally.

To forearm yourself, you may consider familiarising yourself with not only the FCA Latest Publications, but with the various helpful PDFs and guides. Other general areas of interest may be obtained from FCA sector briefings, discussion and consultation papers, the current Financial Risk Outlook, FCA business plan; and Dear CEO letters. In addition, Industry groups, colleagues/contacts in other firms and professional advisors will have a view as to what are the current hot topics.

An important point to remember is that a peer group comparison will be included in the letter, so understanding what types of Firms the FCA will consider as your peers and how you measure up against them will assist in planning for any other visit. Be warned: The FCA allocated Peer group may not include who you think - peer groups can be allocated by business mix, location or the FCA regulatory remit.

A common misconception appears to be that the FCA are limited to the information and material provided by the firm at the time of the documentation request. In fact, their sources of information are varied and can include any previous Risk Mitigation Plans (and progress made on implementation of these), ICARA/ICAS reviews.

This along with any Internal Capital Guidance letters, the FCA relationship manager (if any), whistle-blower claims, internet searches, social media (Facebook, Twitter, Digg etc.) as well as senior management who have previously been involved in reviews or have otherwise interacted with the FCA, will provide some insight into the specific area of concern for the Firm in the upcoming review. There is always the intelligence provided by the general public and industry professionals who may come across something and report it to the regulator.

Preparing for the Review

Avoiding surprises

If, during the pre-visit planning, there are weaknesses identified or even breaches or any other red flags, how will these be dealt with? Senior managers should be aware of any and all action points either raised previously by the FCA or identified by the firm as part of its ongoing monitoring, and the work done to rectify the issues.

Correct ownership must be taken and steps taken to demonstrate the issue is under active management and evidence of ongoing resolution should be to hand. It is important to show that this is being treated as business as usual, not as a one off for the visit. A strong risk culture with Risk and Compliance fully engaged throughout the business.

Increasingly important is the role that Management Information (MI) has to play in the running of regulated firms today.

You need to be able to ensure that senior managers can justify the content, inherent assumptions and frequency of MI in order to be able to demonstrate that it is effective and fit for purpose. In addition, firms should be able to show how MI is generated and then used to drive decisions and actions.

There should be a clear definition of key elements of how the business is run and managed.

- the strategic priorities for the business;
- the main risks to the firm and how they are identified;
- how risk appetite is determined;
- the challenge processes that are built into the risk framework;
- how the effectiveness of the corporate governance framework is assessed;
- how the firm knows that it is treating customers fairly;
- how the culture of the firm would be described;
- operation and effectiveness of the risk, compliance and audit functions providing lines of defence; and
- what could make the firm fail and what are the indicators and mitigating factors.

With all the preparation in the world, the outcome is crucially dependent on ensuring that interviewees provide clear, accurate information about the areas on which they have knowledge. The interviewees should feel comfortable in commenting that they do not work in an area or have no working knowledge if they really don't.

The areas they have knowledge or competency in they should be easily able to comment and effectively demonstrate the controls within the firm.

Confirm with the FCA Team coordinator if they wish or will permit a member of compliance to also attend the interviews, and if so, ensure that you have a suitably senior and knowledgeable member of the department available for the more senior, if not all of the interviews. Anyone who may be selected for interview should:

- Give clear, brief answers
- Stick to the remit of their role and not try to guess or answer wider questions if unsure.
- They should avoid letting personal opinions or ego get in the way of factual answers.
- Be able to evidence that major decisions, e.g., around strategy and risk appetite, are being discussed at board meetings and effectively challenged rather than simply rubber-stamped.
- If they are not senior management, they should be able to explain how decisions are disseminated through the firm.

- Don't use unfamiliar terminology: if they don't know, ask what is meant.

Executives need to be able to explain and demonstrate how the firm's governance process works and more specifically articulate the level of risk appetite and how this affects business decisions.

Executives should also show awareness and be able to explain clearly what elements or events could bring the business down and what is being done to offset those risks.

Compliance Consultant (info@complianceconsultant.org) provides an executive training program and this can sometimes be provided as a crash course if needed.

This is not a memory test, notebooks or other documents can be taken in with you.

All interviewees would do well to use the meeting with the FCA as an opportunity to demonstrate how they have correctly and accurately discharged the obligations of their role. While this is obviously critical for approved persons it sets a strong example at all levels of the firm.
It would be worth noting that if an individual interviewee is unavailable on the required day, the FCA may conduct the interview later at its Canary Wharf offices, which can be more stressful.

The Visit - What is expected

Your project team, and indeed all staff, by the dawning of the first day of the visit, should be able to articulate the desired outcome of the review visit and the firm's key messages to the FCA.

Organisation and smooth running, provision of extra information and timeliness of persons appearing for interview is essential during the visit to ensure that the review can be undertaken as quickly and smoothly as possible.
This is so often overlooked by many firms and can be easily facilitated.

A good idea is to;

- Consider assigning an administrative manager for the visit to keep executives on time for interviews, arrange for the provision of files, refreshments, photocopying, access to systems and to act as general liaison point between the firm and the FCA visit team. An office manager or team leader would be best suited: who know not only the system but who to contact when it doesn't work.
- Ensure availability of significant people for interview.
- Book interview rooms and a secure room for the FCA to work in.

As previously explained it is important that you maintain records of information that you have provided to the regulator and as part of this it is advisable to keep records of meetings and interviews that take place as part of the visit. The FCA will normally allow note-takers to attend the meetings, but you should confirm that this is permitted and ask about the acceptability of using recording equipment, if it is considered applicable.

On a daily basis you should seek to have a daily debrief with the FCA and circulate the results to senior managers. It may also be possible to provide updates in the gaps between the FCA interviews.

As we have seen over the last few months, the FCA has been placing much more emphasis on the role of senior management in its reviews. The outcomes-focussed regulatory approach represents less reliance on systems and controls as the days when the FCA relied on management to make the right judgement have long gone. Today the FCA will question the judgement and rationale of decisions of senior managers and take action if their actions have led to unacceptable risks.

Executives and Non-Executive Directors are expected to not only be able to articulate clearly how governance structures work across the organisation but how these structures are appropriate and effective in the Firm's model and how they personally provide an active challenge to management, preferably with examples. For smaller companies the emphasis is on risk appraisal, risk mitigation and controls.

As you may have gathered, advisers are not the prime candidates for interviews these days and there appears to be not only an increased number but also a much wider range of interviewees such as the role and effectiveness of Non-Executive Directors and a move to include junior level personnel in any interviews.

Administration staff may also be questioned about a variety of issues and operational challenges they encounter on a day-to-day basis.

Increasingly the scope of interviews is also becoming much widely reported.

The FCA wants to see a firm which is capable of realistically assessing risks facing it from all quarters, the effective and timely reporting on those risks and their proposed or actual mitigation.
The FCA is very likely to be interested in how you, as a company, define risk appetite and places risks in the context of that risk appetite. The FCA will want to see a firm which is not afraid to identify and escalate deficiencies or problems, employ speedy and expert advice, willing to discuss solutions and monitor delivery of those solutions and, in particular, is willing and able to learn from mistakes.

Key Points for Consideration

It cannot be reiterated enough or too often that for you to obtain the best result from any regulatory review or any themed visit, briefings and mock interviews with individual coaching and feedback are among the best tools that can be used to assist the individuals to successfully engage with the FCA.

Typically, this process would be led by Compliance and may involve the use of outside compliance and risk solution consultants (as a fresh set of eyes and to provide an objective viewpoint and additional experiential information). Individuals should be able to address risks and issues not only in their area of direct responsibility but also in their role as a manager of a business area or function and as a member of the leadership team, boards and committees. They should be able to reconcile these roles within a Firm-wide view of the Risk Management Process providing evidence and examples where possible.

Preparation should not ignore simple interview techniques - body language and attitude can impact how the interview proceeds. For some individuals the interview process can be intimidating - simple coaching and prior preparation can go a long way to relieve anxiety.

Do agree on the presence of note-takers in advance. These individuals should be able to quickly identify emerging key points/possible areas of concern, and their role should be to identify issues as the review process progresses, brief management and prepare those yet to be interviewed. Note takers should have a close of day de-brief with the project team. At the conclusion of the visit a Firm should ask for a close out meeting assess initial reactions, clear up any factual inaccuracies and determine whether any further documentation or interviews are needed.

Whilst the inspection process may not be a welcome one, full cooperation with the FCA team is expected. Firms are encouraged to engage with the FCA in a proactive and open-minded matter (Principle 11). The inspection team should be provided with interview rooms, and a space to work with access to telephone, refreshments, and access to copying facilities as well as any systems to view documents "online".

The FCA will have a team of two or often more people. FCA Specialists are often called in to drill down (Deep Dive) in a particular area and scrutinise a Firm's business activities and risk management practices. The FCA may have two teams on site at any one time, with one conducting interviews while the other makes notes of completed interviews and prepares for the next. In some cases, enforcement staff have been included and inspection teams have sat in on board meetings and risk committee meetings.

Next Steps

Following the review visit, a Firm should agree with the FCA the timing of the FCA follow up and clarify its understanding of the messages given; agreeing on what the on-going communication with the FCA should be up to the receipt of the draft report letter.

A draft Risk Mitigation Programme (RMP) will normally be drawn up by the FCA team and you should be sure to ask for a copy to ensure that any factual inaccuracies within the RMP can be followed up.

You may wish to consider appointing a RMP resolution manager to oversee the coordination of the activities, responsibilities and reporting to the FCA, or if you are a SME then the Compliance Officer will normally fulfil this function. There should follow a specific full board discussion on the issues raised and the resources required for remediation.

It may be a good idea to invite a compliance consultancy to attend the discussion to take notes and offer advice on any rectification actions needed. This is often frowned upon for routine meetings. A lot of the work will be easily undertaken internally, but it is important to deal with the issues as a whole rather than separate non-cohesive elements.

A vitally important part of the RMP process is to keep and maintain a full documentary record of all actions taken, together with the responsible, agreed timescales for correcting issues and supporting evidence to show that new and fully functioning controls have been put in place, or existing controls have been improved, to prevent any issue identified from recurring.

If you are a member of a group, or a part of a foreign owned company, you should give due consideration to external notification of head offices, parent companies and overseas regulators, where applicable, the results of the visit and a follow up remedial action plan if necessary. Before the dust settles, but after everyone has had a chance to exhale and reflect on their experience, hold a workshop (on or offsite) and review the visit and of what went well and any lessons to be learned.

Once received, the draft letter should be reviewed for factual accuracy, and evidence provided where this is not the case – this is the only part of the letter a Firm is allowed to comment on and can influence after the interview have completed. Firms must ensure that the priorities and issues are clear to them in the Risk Mitigation Program. This should be submitted to the board with a clear plan of action, including resources required, timescales for addressing issues, measures to prevent any issues from re-occurring, and how and what controls will be implemented. All actions will need to be fully documented with regular progress reports put in place.

How Do We Know If We Are Looking at Enforcement Action?

From your daily meetings and your close out meeting you will have a strong feeling of where the RMP is going or the general flavour. Obviously, some areas will require further investigation which will be conducted normally off-site. All evidence (or lack of it) is cited in the report.

The key elements that the FCA use to determine enforcement referral are;

- Has there been actual or potential consumer loss/detriment?
- Is there evidence of financial crime or risk of financial crime?
- Are there actions or potential breaches that could undermine public confidence in the orderliness of financial markets?
- Are there issues that indicate a widespread problem or weakness at the firm/issuer?
- Is there evidence that the firm/issuer/individual has profited from the action or potential breaches?
- Has the firm/issuer/individual failed to bring the actions or potential breaches to the attention of the FCA?
- Is the issue to be referred relevant to an FCA strategic priority?
- If the issue does not fall within an FCA strategic priority, does the conduct in question make the conduct particularly egregious and presenting a serious risk to one of the FCA's objectives?
- What was the reaction of the firm/issuer/individual to the breach?
- Overall, is the use of the enforcement tool likely to further the FCA's aims and Objectives?

- Does the suspected misconduct involve an overseas jurisdiction? If so, would enforcement action materially further investor protection or market confidence in that jurisdiction?

What can they do about it?

- Financial penalties and public censures
- Private warnings
- Variation and cancellation of Part IV permission
- Prohibition orders and withdrawal of approval
- Suspensions
- Injunctive action
- Restitution and redress
- Criminal prosecution
- Insolvency
- Collective Investment Schemes
- Disqualification of auditors and actuaries
- Disapplication orders against members of the professions
- Cancellation of Sponsor approval
- Non-FSMA powers

In most cases where a lack of controls are found, or there are minor breaches and bad practices a period of enhanced supervision is recommended with regular reporting to the FCA and a significant increase on management time and focus.

The next stage could easily be a specific S166 Report on a designated area of suspect operation. Don't forget that under Part XI of the FSMA, a Section 166 Skilled Person's Reports can be used, in the FCA's examples in SUP 5 Annex 1 for a single or any mix of;

- Diagnostic
- Diagnostic / monitoring
- Monitoring
- Preventative
- Remedial

These are not restricted to the firm today either. The Report can cover;

- all firms (all authorised persons under section 31 FSMA)
- any other member of the firm's group
- a partnership of which the firm is a member
- a person who has at any relevant time been a person falling within the above (where such person was carrying on a business)

In this overview we have offered a number of common-sense tips on how to improve the chances of both the Firm as a whole and individuals in obtaining their objectives for a successful outcome from a regulatory review visit, whether as part of a wider thematic review or a Deep Dive.

Early preparation is important to ensure that you are totally ready for the visit, with sound Governance and Risk Management arrangements in place.

Appointing a project team with clear responsibilities within the context of a clearly articulated and understood objective for success as well as ongoing dialogue between that team and the FCA are also important if your organisation allows that level of resource. Finally, proper preparation (briefings. mock interviews, feedback) are also tried and tested ways of maximising the likelihood of success. Although we cannot cater for all models and sizes of business, we hope this has provided you with a more thorough insight into what is involved.

In summary; whenever you are dealing with any compliance event, breach or issue, or if you are subject to regulatory scrutiny, consider the following areas.

- Take control of the problem in so far as possible
- Analyse the issue – but do so with the benefit of legal advice
- Privilege and protected items S413 – the role of compliance
- Do not create hostages to fortune – the dangers of email and text messages
- Take action to ensure problem cannot recur
- Review systems and controls
- Consider remediation/compensation of customer losses
- Consider disciplinary action against employees – but consider consequences carefully. Dismissal may deprive you of access to important information
- Consider the need for employees to have separate advice and fund that advice
- Show FCA you are being pro-active in dealing with the issue

- Try to stay one step ahead of the FCA by anticipating their requirements
- Other investigations/litigation and their outcomes.

Conclusion

Preparation for a regulatory visit is essential. Do not try to wing it. If you need someone to oversee and arrange the preparation for you, independently and not emotionally involved, contact **Compliance Consultant** (info@complianceconsultant.org**). Email** info@complianceconsultant.org **or call 0800 689 0190.**

Chapter 17: Consumer Duty: A New Era in Financial Services Regulation

The Financial Conduct Authority (FCA) introduced the Consumer Duty as a transformative regulatory framework aimed at setting higher and clearer standards of consumer protection across the financial services sector. This chapter explores the key aspects of the Consumer Duty, its implementation timeline, and the implications for firms operating in the UK financial services industry. The rules were implemented from 31st July 2023.

Overview of the Consumer Duty

The Consumer Duty represents a significant shift in the regulatory landscape, requiring firms to put their customers' needs first and focus on delivering good outcomes. It goes beyond the previous principles-based approach, setting more specific expectations for firms in their dealings with retail customers.

Key Components

The Consumer Duty comprises three main elements:

1. The Consumer Principle: This overarching principle requires firms to act to deliver good outcomes for retail customers.

2. The Cross-cutting Rules: These rules require firms to:

- Act in good faith towards retail customers
- Avoid foreseeable harm to retail customers
- Enable and support retail customers to pursue their financial objectives

3. The Four Outcomes: These specific outcomes focus on key elements of the firm-customer relationship:

- Products and services
- Price and value
- Consumer understanding
- Consumer support

The Consumer Principle

The Consumer Principle, which states that "A firm must act to deliver good outcomes for retail customers," sits at the heart of the Consumer Duty. This principle sets a higher standard than the existing Treating Customers Fairly (TCF) principle, requiring firms to be proactive in their approach to customer outcomes.

Implications for Firms

Firms must:

- Assess and evidence the outcomes their customers are experiencing
- Identify where these outcomes fall short of the new higher standards

- Take action to address any shortcomings

The Cross-cutting Rules

The cross-cutting rules provide more specific guidance on how firms should approach their obligations under the Consumer Duty.

Acting in Good Faith

Firms must conduct themselves honestly, fairly, and openly in their dealings with customers. This includes:

- Being transparent about products and services
- Avoiding conflicts of interest
- Not exploiting customer vulnerabilities or behavioural biases

Avoiding Foreseeable Harm

Firms are expected to proactively identify and mitigate potential sources of harm to customers. This involves:

- Conducting thorough risk assessments
- Implementing robust controls and monitoring systems
- Taking prompt action when issues are identified

Enabling and Supporting Customers

Firms should empower customers to make informed decisions about financial products and services. This includes:

- Providing clear and timely information
- Offering appropriate support throughout the customer journey
- Ensuring products and services meet customer needs and objectives

The Four Outcomes

The four outcomes provide a framework for firms to assess whether they are meeting the Consumer Duty standards in key areas of their business.

Products and Services

Firms must ensure that their products and services are designed to meet the needs, characteristics, and objectives of a specific target market. This involves:

- Conducting thorough market research and customer analysis
- Regularly reviewing product performance and suitability
- Making necessary adjustments to products or target markets

Price and Value

Firms must ensure that their products and services provide fair value to customers. This requires:

- Assessing the overall cost of products and services against the benefits provided
- Considering the needs and characteristics of the target market

- Ensuring pricing structures are transparent and do not exploit customer vulnerabilities

Consumer Understanding

Firms must communicate in a way that enables consumers to make informed decisions. This includes:

- Using clear, fair, and not misleading language
- Tailoring communications to the target audience
- Providing information at appropriate times in the customer journey

Consumer Support

Firms must provide a level of support that meets customer needs throughout their relationship. This involves:

- Offering multiple channels for customer support
- Ensuring staff are adequately trained and empowered to assist customers
- Providing additional support for vulnerable customers

Governance and Accountability

The Consumer Duty places significant emphasis on the role of senior management in ensuring compliance.

Board Responsibilities

Boards must:

- Approve an implementation plan for the Consumer Duty
- Ensure the duty is embedded into the firm's culture
- Regularly review and challenge data on customer outcomes

Champion Role

Firms must appoint a Consumer Duty Champion at board level (or equivalent governing body) to ensure that the duty remains central to the firm's purpose, strategy, and culture.

Monitoring and Evidencing Compliance

Firms are expected to monitor, test, and evidence their compliance with the Consumer Duty on an ongoing basis.

Data and Management Information

Firms should:

- Collect and analyse relevant data on customer outcomes
- Develop key performance indicators (KPIs) aligned with the Consumer Duty
- Regularly report on compliance to senior management and the board

Annual Board Report

Firms must produce an annual report assessing their compliance with the Consumer Duty. This report should:

- Summarise the results of monitoring activities
- Identify any areas for improvement
- Set out actions taken or planned to address issues

Implications for Different Sectors

While the Consumer Duty applies across the financial services industry, its impact may vary depending on the sector.

Banking

Banks will need to focus on:

- Ensuring fair pricing across product ranges
- Improving customer communications, particularly around terms and conditions
- Enhancing support for vulnerable customers, including those in financial difficulty

Insurance

Insurers will need to consider:

- Product design and suitability for target markets
- Claims handling processes and outcomes
- Value assessments, particularly for add-on products

Investments and Wealth Management

Firms in this sector should focus on:

- Ensuring investment products and strategies align with customer risk profiles and objectives
- Improving transparency around fees and charges
- Enhancing customer understanding of investment risks and potential outcomes

Challenges and Opportunities

The implementation of the Consumer Duty presents both challenges and opportunities for firms.

Challenges

- Significant resource requirements for implementation and ongoing compliance
- Potential need for cultural change within organisations
- Complexity in assessing and evidencing good customer outcomes

Opportunities

- Improved customer trust and loyalty
- Potential for product and service innovation
- Enhanced reputation and competitive advantage

Consumer Duty Alignment

To align their company purpose with the Consumer Duty, firms need to make several key adaptations:

1. **Prioritise customer outcomes**: Firms should reframe their purpose to explicitly focus on delivering good outcomes for customers, rather than solely on profit or growth. This means putting customer interests at the heart of business strategy and decision-making.

2. **Embed customer-centricity in culture**: The company purpose should reflect a cultural shift towards customer-centricity across the entire organisation. This involves aligning values, behaviours, and incentives to support good customer outcomes.

3. **Emphasise proactive harm prevention**: The purpose should highlight the firm's commitment to proactively identifying and mitigating potential sources of customer harm, rather than just reacting to issues.

4. **Focus on long-term value creation**: Firms should articulate a purpose that balances short-term profitability with long-term value creation for customers and the business.

5. **Promote transparency and accountability**: The purpose should emphasise the firm's commitment to being transparent about products, services, and pricing, as well as taking accountability for customer outcomes.

6. **Highlight fair value**: Firms should incorporate the concept of providing fair value to customers into their purpose, ensuring products and services offer genuine benefits relative to their cost.

7. Emphasise customer support: The purpose should reflect a commitment to providing high-quality, accessible customer support throughout the customer journey.

8. Promote financial inclusion: Firms may want to include a focus on serving diverse customer needs and promoting financial inclusion as part of their purpose.

9. Align with regulatory expectations: The purpose should explicitly acknowledge the firm's commitment to meeting and exceeding regulatory expectations, particularly those set out in the Consumer Duty.

10. Emphasise continuous improvement: Firms should incorporate a commitment to ongoing learning, improvement, and innovation in service of customer outcomes into their purpose.

By adapting their company purpose in these ways, firms can demonstrate a genuine commitment to the principles of the Consumer Duty and set the tone for its implementation throughout the organisation. This alignment of purpose with regulatory expectations can help drive the cultural and operational changes needed to fully embed the Consumer Duty into the firm's practices.

Integration Into Existing Governance

Based on regulatory guidance, here are some key-ways firms can integrate the Consumer Duty into their existing governance structures:

1. Appoint a Consumer Duty Champion at board level or equivalent governing body. This champion should support the Chair and CEO in raising the Duty in relevant discussions and challenge management on embedding the Duty and focusing on consumer outcomes.

2. Ensure the board regularly considers and challenges the extent to which the firm is delivering good consumer outcomes. Board discussions should include detailed minutes evidencing the nature of discussions, challenges, and remedial actions required.

3. Develop robust governance frameworks with clear executive accountability for Duty implementation and board oversight. This includes scrutiny and challenge from audit and risk functions.

4. Provide regular summary management information (MI) to the board aligned to each of the 4 Consumer Duty outcomes. This MI should include RAG-rated measures with clear conclusions, identified shortfalls, mitigating actions, and responsible owners.

5. Integrate the Duty into the firm's risk management framework, with regular reviews by risk and compliance functions.

6. Ensure internal audit includes Consumer Duty compliance in its audit plan and provides independent assurance to the board.

7. Align remuneration and incentive policies with delivering good consumer outcomes. Review and challenge whether existing policies could lead to foreseeable harm.

8. Embed Consumer Duty considerations into product governance processes, including regular reviews of existing products and services.

9. Integrate the Duty into the firm's culture and strategy. Consider altering the company purpose to signal that staff actions and behaviours should focus on customer outcomes.

10. Reflect the Consumer Duty in the Senior Managers and Certification Regime (SMCR). Allocate the new Duty of Responsibility to an appropriate senior manager.

11. Implement an annual board assessment process to review Duty implementation and compliance, identifying risks, poor outcomes, and required actions.

12. Ensure governance structures extend to oversight of third parties and distribution chains where relevant to Duty compliance.

13. Develop data strategies and management information systems to monitor, measure and evidence consumer outcomes on an ongoing basis.

By integrating these elements into existing governance structures, firms can create a comprehensive framework for embedding the Consumer Duty throughout their organisation and ensuring ongoing compliance.

Conclusion

The Consumer Duty represents a significant evolution in the UK's financial services regulatory framework. By placing customer outcomes at the centre of firms' strategies and operations, it aims to foster a financial services industry that truly serves the needs of its customers. While implementation may have presented challenges, firms that successfully embed the Consumer Duty into their culture and practices stand to benefit from improved customer relationships and a stronger, more sustainable business model.

As the industry continues to adapt to these new requirements, ongoing dialogue between firms, regulators, and consumers will be crucial in ensuring that the Consumer Duty achieves its intended objectives and delivers tangible benefits to retail customers across the UK financial services sector.

Chapter 18: Vulnerable Customers

In recent years, the fair treatment of vulnerable customers has become a key priority for the Financial Conduct Authority (FCA) in the United Kingdom. This chapter will explore the concept of customer vulnerability, the FCA's guidance on this topic, and the practical steps firms can take to ensure they are meeting their obligations to protect and support vulnerable individuals.

Defining Vulnerability

The FCA defines a vulnerable customer as "someone who, due to their personal circumstances, is especially susceptible to harm, particularly when a firm is not acting with appropriate levels of care". It's important to note that vulnerability can be temporary, sporadic, or permanent, and can affect individuals across all demographics and socioeconomic backgrounds.

The Scale of Vulnerability

Research conducted by the FCA has revealed that vulnerability is far more prevalent than many might assume. As of January 2024, approximately 7.4 million people in the UK were struggling to pay their bills and credit repayments, highlighting the ongoing impact of the cost-of-living crisis. Moreover, the FCA estimates that up to 50% of people will be considered vulnerable at some point in their lifetime.

Drivers of Vulnerability

The FCA has identified four key drivers of vulnerability:

1. **Health**: Physical disabilities, severe or long-term illness, mental health conditions, and addictions.

2. **Life events**: Significant life changes such as bereavement, job loss, relationship breakdown, or caring responsibilities.

3. **Resilience**: Low ability to withstand financial or emotional shocks due to low savings, over-indebtedness, or low emotional resilience.

4. **Capability**: Low knowledge of financial matters, poor literacy or numeracy skills, or low confidence in managing money.

FCA Guidance on the Fair Treatment of Vulnerable Customers

In February 2021, the FCA published its finalised guidance for firms on the fair treatment of vulnerable customers. This guidance aims to drive improvements in the way firms treat vulnerable consumers and bring about a practical shift in firms' actions and behaviour.

The guidance is structured around four key areas:

1. Understanding the needs of vulnerable customers
2. Skills and capability of staff
3. Taking practical action
4. Monitoring and evaluation

Let's explore each of these areas in more detail.

1. Understanding the Needs of Vulnerable Customers

Firms are expected to:

- Understand the nature and scale of characteristics of vulnerability that exist in their target market and customer base.
- Comprehend the impact of vulnerability on the needs of consumers, including the types of harm or disadvantage customers may be vulnerable to and how this might affect their experience and outcomes.

To achieve this, firms can:

- Utilise published information from reputable sources such as the FCA, charities, trade bodies, and professional organisations to understand the drivers of vulnerability and their impact on financial services engagement.
- Conduct research within their own customer base to identify vulnerable groups and their specific needs.

2. Skills and Capability of Staff

The FCA emphasises the importance of:

- Embedding the fair treatment of vulnerable consumers across the workforce.

- Ensuring frontline staff have the necessary skills and capability to recognise and respond to a range of vulnerability characteristics.
- Offering practical and emotional support to frontline staff dealing with vulnerable consumers.

Practical steps firms can take include:

- Implementing comprehensive training programmes on vulnerability, including specialised sessions such as the Alzheimer's Society Dementia Friends programme.
- Recruiting for and encouraging listening skills, emotional intelligence, and empathy among staff.
- Creating an environment where staff feel empowered to have difficult conversations and respond empathetically to vulnerable customers.

3. Taking Practical Action

This area focuses on product and service design, customer service, and communications.

Product and Service Design:

- Consider the potential negative impacts of products or services on vulnerable consumers.
- Take vulnerable consumers into account at all stages of the product and service design process.

- Design products and services to avoid potential harmful impacts.

Customer Service:

- Set up systems and processes that support and enable vulnerable consumers to disclose their needs.
- Deliver flexible customer service that responds to the needs of vulnerable consumers.
- Make consumers aware of available support, including options for third-party representation and specialist support services.

Communications:

- Ensure all communications and information about products and services are understandable for consumers in the target market and customer base.
- Consider how to communicate with vulnerable consumers, taking into account their needs.
- Offer multiple communication channels to give vulnerable consumers a choice.

4. Monitoring and Evaluation

Firms should:

- Monitor and assess whether they are meeting and responding to the needs of customers with characteristics of vulnerability.
- Make improvements where they are not meeting these needs.

This can involve:

- Collecting and analysing data on vulnerable customers and their outcomes.
- Regularly reviewing and updating policies and procedures related to vulnerable customers.
- Conducting internal audits to ensure compliance with vulnerability guidelines.

Practical Examples and Case Studies

To illustrate how firms can effectively support vulnerable customers, let's consider some real-world examples:

Case Study 1: Irrational Pension Withdrawals

An adviser noticed that a couple had requested large pension withdrawals shortly after one of them had been diagnosed with cancer. Recognising that the clients might be making irrational decisions due to stress, the adviser worked with Fidelity to reverse the withdrawals and reinvest the funds. This case demonstrates the importance of staff being alert to signs of vulnerability and taking proactive steps to protect clients' interests.

Case Study 2: Flexible Approach to Bank Details

An attorney holding a Court of Protection order for a client with a brain injury needed to make a withdrawal to pay the client's tax bill.

However, the bank details were initially rejected as they were in the attorney's name rather than the client's. By working with their Vulnerable Customer and Bereavement teams, Fidelity was able to adapt their processes to accept the attorney's bank details, ensuring the client's needs were met while maintaining proper safeguards.

Case Study 3: Adapting Processes for Junior ISAs

When an adviser attempted to open a Junior ISA for a 17-year-old client with a Court of Protection order, the application was initially rejected due to standard signature requirements.

This case prompted Fidelity to review and update their processes to accommodate Junior ISAs for customers with Court of Protection orders, demonstrating how firms can learn from individual cases to improve their overall approach to vulnerability.

The Role of Technology and Data

As firms strive to improve their treatment of vulnerable customers, many are turning to technology and data analytics to enhance their capabilities. The FCA's survey of firms includes questions about the use of Artificial Intelligence (AI) and big data in approaches to vulnerable customers.

While technology can offer significant benefits, such as improved identification of vulnerability indicators and more personalised support, firms must be cautious about potential risks. These might include:

- Privacy concerns and data protection issues
- The risk of algorithmic bias
- Over-reliance on automated systems at the expense of human judgement and empathy

Firms should strive to strike a balance between leveraging technological advancements and maintaining a human-centric approach to vulnerability.

Regulatory Expectations and Enforcement

The FCA has made it clear that the fair treatment of vulnerable customers is not just a matter of good practice, but a regulatory requirement. Firms that fail to meet these standards may face enforcement action and financial penalties.

In April 2024, the FCA announced a review of firms' treatment of vulnerable customers, including their understanding of consumer needs, the skills and capability of staff, and standards of customer service. This review underscores the regulator's ongoing commitment to this issue and serves as a reminder to firms of the importance of having robust frameworks in place to protect vulnerable consumers.

Main Challenges

Based on regulatory guidance, some of the main challenges firms face in identifying and supporting vulnerable customers include:

1. Accurately identifying vulnerable customers:

- Many customers may not self-identify as vulnerable or disclose their circumstances.
- Vulnerability can be temporary, fluctuating or permanent, making it difficult to track.
- There's often a disconnect between the proportion of vulnerable customers firms identify versus what regulators expect.

2. Data gaps and system constraints:

- Legacy systems may restrict firms' ability to record and track vulnerabilities, especially transient ones.
- Firms may have incomplete data on existing customers, particularly for closed products.

3. Defining vulnerability appropriately:

- The FCA's broad definition can make it challenging for firms to operationalise.
- Firms need to develop workable definitions focused on their specific target market and customer base.

4. Encouraging disclosure:

- Customers may be reluctant to disclose vulnerabilities, especially to product providers they don't interact with regularly.
- Firms need to build trust and provide opportunities for disclosure across channels.

5. Staff training and capabilities:

- Ensuring frontline staff have the skills to recognize and respond to various vulnerability characteristics.
- Providing practical and emotional support to staff dealing with vulnerable customers.

6. Product and service design:

- Considering the needs of vulnerable customers throughout the product lifecycle.
- Ensuring products sold to closed book customers remain appropriate as circumstances change.

7. Flexible customer service:

- Adapting processes and communication channels to meet diverse needs of vulnerable customers.
- Providing support through multiple channels.

8. Monitoring outcomes:

- Developing appropriate metrics and management information to track outcomes for vulnerable customer groups.
- Addressing data gaps that hinder effective monitoring.

9. Balancing data protection with information sharing:

- Sharing relevant vulnerability information across teams while respecting privacy.

10. Senior leadership engagement:

- Ensuring vulnerability is championed at the highest levels and embedded throughout the organisation.

11. Addressing disengaged or "gone-away" customers:

- Identifying and re-engaging with customers of closed products who may have become disengaged or cannot be contacted.

12. Fair value assessments:

- Evaluating whether closed products continue to offer fair value, especially for vulnerable customers.

13. Using technology appropriately:

- Leveraging AI and data analytics to identify vulnerability while avoiding over-reliance on automated systems.

Firms need to take a comprehensive approach to address these challenges, including reviewing processes, improving data capabilities, enhancing staff training, and embedding consideration of vulnerability throughout product lifecycles and customer journeys.

Key Legal Implications

Some of the key legal implications for firms that fail to protect customer data privacy include:

1. Financial penalties:

- The Information Commissioner's Office (ICO) can impose fines of up to £17.5 million or 4% of annual global turnover (whichever is higher) for serious violations of data protection laws like GDPR.
- For less severe breaches, fines can be up to £8.7 million or 2% of annual turnover.

2. Regulatory enforcement action:

- The ICO can issue enforcement notices requiring specific actions to comply with data protection laws.
- Firms may face investigations into their data protection practices.
- The ICO can suspend a company's data processing activities if there's a risk to individuals' rights.

3. Legal claims and compensation:

- Affected individuals can seek compensation for damages, distress or financial loss resulting from data breaches.
- Class action lawsuits are possible for large-scale breaches affecting many customers.

4. Reputational damage:

- Data breaches can severely damage a firm's reputation, erode customer trust, and lead to loss of business.
- Rebuilding trust after a major breach can be extremely difficult and costly.

5. Operational disruption:

- Firms may need to invest in remedial measures, enhanced security, and notifications to affected individuals.
- Business operations can be disrupted while dealing with breach fallout.

6. Increased regulatory scrutiny:

- Firms that suffer breaches are likely to face increased ongoing scrutiny from regulators.

7. Personal liability:

- In some cases, individual executives or employees could face personal liability for serious breaches.

8. Loss of authorisations /licenses:

- For regulated firms, serious breaches could potentially lead to loss of regulatory authorisations or licenses in extreme cases.

The severity of consequences depends on factors like the nature and scale of the breach, the sensitivity of data involved, and the firm's conduct before and after the incident. Having robust data protection measures in place is critical for firms to avoid these serious legal and financial risks.

In Summary

The fair treatment of vulnerable customers is a complex and evolving area of financial regulation in the UK. As the FCA continues to refine its approach and expectations, firms must remain proactive in developing and implementing strategies to identify, support, and protect vulnerable individuals.

By fostering a culture of empathy and understanding, investing in staff training and capabilities, designing products and services with vulnerability in mind, and continuously monitoring and improving their practices, firms can not only meet their regulatory obligations but also build trust and loyalty among their customer base.

As the financial services landscape continues to evolve, particularly in light of ongoing economic challenges and technological advancements, the ability to effectively support vulnerable customers will likely become an increasingly important differentiator for firms in the UK market.

Chapter 19: UK GDPR and the DPA 2018

The United Kingdom General Data Protection Regulation (UK GDPR) and the Data Protection Act 2018 (DPA 2018) form the cornerstone of data protection law in the UK. These regulations have significant implications for financial services firms, requiring them to implement robust data protection measures and ensure compliance with stringent privacy standards.

Overview of UK GDPR

The UK GDPR is the UK's implementation of the General Data Protection Regulation (GDPR), which came into effect on 25 May 2018. Following the UK's departure from the European Union, the GDPR was incorporated into UK law as the UK GDPR, maintaining a high standard of data protection within the country.

Key Principles

The UK GDPR is built upon seven fundamental principles:

1. Lawfulness, fairness, and transparency
2. Purpose limitation
3. Data minimisation
4. Accuracy
5. Storage limitation

6. Integrity and confidentiality (security)
7. Accountability

These principles should be at the heart of an organisation's approach to processing personal data.

Territorial Scope

The UK GDPR applies to:

- Controllers and processors based in the UK
- Controllers and processors outside the UK that offer goods or services to individuals in the UK
- Controllers and processors outside the UK that monitor the behaviour of individuals in the UK

The Data Protection Act 2018

The DPA 2018 complements the UK GDPR and provides additional UK-specific details. It covers areas such as:

- Processing of criminal conviction data
- How intelligence services are permitted to process personal data
- The age at which a young person can consent to their personal data being processed by an 'information society service' (typically social media platforms)

Individual Rights Under UK GDPR

The UK GDPR grants individuals several rights concerning their personal data:

1. **Right to be informed**: Organisations must provide clear and concise information about how they process personal data.

2. **Right of access**: Individuals can request access to their personal data and receive additional information about its processing.

3. **Right to rectification**: Inaccurate or incomplete personal data must be corrected upon request.

4. **Right to erasure**: Also known as the 'right to be forgotten', individuals can request the deletion of their personal data under certain circumstances.

5. **Right to restrict processing**: Individuals can request that an organisation limits the processing of their personal data.

6. **Right to data portability**: Individuals can obtain and reuse their personal data across different services.

7. **Right to object**: Individuals can object to the processing of their personal data in certain situations.

8. Rights related to automated decision making and profiling: Individuals have specific rights when decisions are made solely by automated means without human involvement.

Compliance Requirements for Financial Services Firms

Financial services firms must ensure they comply with both the UK GDPR and the rules set out by the Financial Conduct Authority (FCA). The FCA and the Information Commissioner's Office (ICO) have stated that compliance with the UK GDPR is compatible with the FCA Handbook rules.

Key compliance areas include:

Data Protection Impact Assessments (DPIAs)

Firms must conduct DPIAs for high-risk processing activities. This involves:

- Identifying and assessing privacy risks
- Implementing measures to mitigate these risks
- Documenting the assessment process and outcomes

Appointment of a Data Protection Officer (DPO)

Many financial services firms will be required to appoint a DPO. The DPO's responsibilities include:

- Monitoring compliance with the UK GDPR and other data protection laws

- Advising on data protection obligations
- Acting as a point of contact for data subjects and supervisory authorities

Data Breach Notification

Firms must have procedures in place to detect, report, and investigate personal data breaches. Significant breaches must be reported to the ICO within 72 hours of discovery.

Record of Processing Activities

Organisations must maintain detailed records of their data processing activities, including:

- Purposes of processing
- Categories of personal data processed
- Recipients of personal data
- Data retention periods
- Security measures implemented

International Data Transfers

Post-Brexit, the UK has implemented its own international data transfer regime. The International Data Transfer Agreement (IDTA) is the UK's version of standard contractual clauses, used as a safeguard mechanism for international transfers of personal data.

Enforcement and Penalties

The ICO is responsible for enforcing the UK GDPR and DPA 2018. Penalties for non-compliance can be severe, with maximum fines of £17.5 million or 4% of annual global turnover, whichever is higher.

FCA and ICO Collaboration

The FCA and ICO work closely together to ensure a consistent approach to data protection in the financial services sector. They have a Memorandum of Understanding in place, outlining their formal relationship and commitment to cooperation.

Data Protection in Enforcement Activities

The FCA uses personal data in carrying out its enforcement functions. This includes:

- Identifying and investigating suspected misconduct
- Using deterrent and remedial powers
- Communicating the basis for enforcement actions

The FCA processes personal data for these purposes under Article 6(1)(e) of the UK GDPR (necessary for the performance of a task carried out in the public interest) and Section 8(c) of the DPA 2018.

Practical Steps for Compliance

Financial services firms should take the following steps to ensure compliance:

1. **Conduct a data audit**: Identify what personal data is held, where it comes from, and how it is used.

2. **Review privacy notices**: Ensure they are clear, concise, and provide all required information.

3. **Implement data protection policies**: Develop and maintain comprehensive data protection policies and procedures.

4. **Train staff**: Provide regular training on data protection principles and the firm's specific policies.

5. **Review data sharing agreements**: Ensure all agreements with third parties are UK GDPR compliant.

6. **Implement technical measures**: Use appropriate security measures such as encryption and access controls.

7. **Establish breach response procedures**: Develop a clear process for detecting, reporting, and investigating data breaches.

8. **Conduct regular audits**: Regularly review and update data protection measures to ensure ongoing compliance.

Data Protection Officer – Key Responsibilities

The main responsibilities of a Data Protection Officer (DPO) under the UK GDPR and Data Protection Act 2018 include:

1. Informing and advising the organisation and its employees about their obligations to comply with data protection laws and regulations.

2. Monitoring compliance with data protection laws, including managing internal data protection activities, advising on data protection impact assessments, training staff, and conducting internal audits.

3. Acting as the first point of contact for supervisory authorities (like the ICO) and for individuals whose data is processed (e.g. employees, customers).

4. Reporting to the highest management level of the organisation.

5. Operating independently and not being dismissed or penalized for performing their tasks.

6. Assisting in monitoring internal compliance with data protection regulations.

7. Providing advice regarding Data Protection Impact Assessments (DPIAs).

8. Cooperating with the supervisory authority (ICO in the UK).

9. Taking into account the risk associated with processing operations, considering the nature, scope, context and purposes of processing.

10. Helping the organisation demonstrate compliance and accountability.

11. Reviewing and updating relevant policies and procedures related to data protection.

12. Overseeing data sharing agreements and processor agreements.

13. Managing communication related to data protection issues.

14. Maintaining required documentation like Records of Processing Activities (RoPA), breach registers, etc.

The DPO must have expert knowledge of data protection law and practices, and the ability to fulfil these tasks independently. They can be an internal employee or externally appointed, as long as there are no conflicts of interest with their other duties.

How Does A DPO Manage a Data Breach?

The key responsibilities and actions of a Data Protection Officer (DPO) in managing a data breach:

1. Pre-incident preparedness:

- Implement data protection by design and default principles.
- Set up monitoring and detection systems to identify potential breaches early.
- Develop comprehensive incident response plans.
- Ensure staff are trained to recognize and report security incidents.

2. When a breach occurs:

- Assess the severity of the breach and determine if it needs to be reported to authorities.
- Coordinate the organisation's response, working with IT, legal, communications and other relevant departments.
- Ensure the breach is contained and mitigated quickly.

3. Reporting and notification:

- Notify the relevant supervisory authority (e.g. ICO in the UK) within 72 hours of becoming aware of a reportable breach.
- Provide required information about the breach to authorities.
- Determine if affected individuals need to be notified and coordinate that communication.

4. Investigation and documentation:

- Facilitate investigation into the root causes of the breach.
- Ensure all aspects of the breach and response are thoroughly documented.

5. Recovery and lessons learned:

- Advise on measures to prevent similar incidents in the future.
- Conduct a post-incident review to assess the response and identify improvements.
- Analyse breach reports over time to understand trends and themes.

6. Communication:

- Act as the point of contact for data subjects and supervisory authorities regarding the breach.
- Manage internal and external communications about the breach, ensuring accuracy and transparency.

7. Ongoing monitoring:

- Continue to monitor compliance and effectiveness of data protection measures.
- Provide regular reports and updates to senior management.

The DPO plays a crucial role in coordinating all aspects of breach response, from detection through recovery, while ensuring compliance with data protection regulations throughout the process. Their independence and expertise are vital in managing breaches effectively and minimising their impact on both the organisation and affected individuals.

Effective Data Breach Incident Response Plan

An effective incident response plan for data breaches include:

1. Preparation and Team Structure:

- Establish a dedicated incident response team with clearly defined roles and responsibilities.
- Include members from IT, legal, HR, PR, and other relevant departments.
- Conduct regular training and simulation exercises.

2. Detection and Identification:

- Implement tools and processes to quickly detect unusual activity.
- Train staff to recognize security incidents and data breaches.
- Establish clear reporting protocols.

3. Assessment and Reporting:

- Have procedures to assess the likelihood and severity of risk to individuals.
- Establish a process for notifying relevant authorities (e.g. ICO) within required timeframes.
- Document reasons if deciding not to report a breach.

4. Containment and Response:

- Develop specific containment strategies for different types of incidents.
- Include procedures for isolating affected systems and preserving evidence.

- Have a clear communication plan for internal and external stakeholders.

5. Eradication and Recovery:

- Outline steps for removing threats and recovering affected systems.
- Include procedures for restoring services and data from backups.
- Define criteria for determining when systems are safe to bring back online.

6. Notification:

- Establish procedures for notifying affected individuals when required.
- Provide clear, plain language communication about the breach and its consequences.
- Offer guidance on how individuals can protect themselves.

7. Post-Incident Analysis:

- Conduct a thorough review of the incident and response.
- Identify lessons learned and areas for improvement.
- Update the incident response plan based on findings.

8. Documentation and Monitoring:

- Maintain detailed logs of all incidents, including near-misses.
- Monitor trends in incidents over time.
- Review and analyse breach reports to prevent recurrences.

9. Continuous Improvement:

- Regularly review and update the incident response plan.
- Conduct ongoing training and awareness programs.
- Stay informed about evolving threats and best practices.

An effective plan should be comprehensive, well-documented, regularly tested, and adaptable to different types of data breaches. It should also align with relevant regulatory requirements and industry standards.

Using AI Anomaly Detection

AI-driven anomaly detection can significantly enhance incident response in several ways:

1. Faster threat detection:

- AI systems can continuously monitor vast amounts of network traffic, log data, and user behaviour in real-time.
- Machine learning algorithms can quickly identify subtle anomalies and deviations from normal patterns that may indicate a security incident.
- This allows for much faster detection of potential threats compared to manual analysis.

2. Improved accuracy:

- AI models can learn from historical data to establish baselines of normal behaviour.

- This allows them to more accurately distinguish between benign anomalies and actual security threats.
- AI can reduce false positives and help security teams focus on genuine incidents.

3. Detection of unknown threats:

- Traditional signature-based detection struggles with zero-day attacks and novel threats.
- AI anomaly detection can potentially identify new, previously unseen attack patterns.
- This provides protection against emerging threats that may bypass conventional security controls.

4. Automated triage and prioritization:

- AI systems can automatically analyse detected anomalies and assign risk scores.
- This helps prioritise incidents based on potential impact and urgency.
- Security teams can focus their efforts on the most critical threats first.

5. Context-aware analysis:

- AI can correlate anomalies across multiple data sources and systems.
- This provides a more holistic view of potential security incidents.
- Contextual analysis helps determine the scope and severity of threats more accurately.

6. Continuous learning and adaptation:

- AI models can continuously learn from new data and feedback.
- This allows them to adapt to evolving threats and changing network environments.
- The system becomes more effective over time at detecting anomalies.

7. Scalability:

- AI can process and analyse massive volumes of data that would be impractical for human analysts.
- This allows for comprehensive monitoring across large, complex networks.

8. Automated response:

- AI systems can trigger automated incident response actions when anomalies are detected.
- This may include isolating affected systems, blocking malicious traffic, or initiating other containment measures.
- Automated responses can significantly reduce the time to mitigate threats.

9. Enhanced forensics and investigation:

- AI can help reconstruct the sequence of events leading to an incident.
- Machine learning can identify patterns and relationships in large datasets to support root cause analysis.

10. Predictive capabilities:

- Advanced AI models may be able to predict potential future incidents based on current anomalies and trends.
- This allows for more proactive threat mitigation.

By leveraging AI-driven anomaly detection, organisations can significantly improve their incident response capabilities - detecting threats faster, responding more effectively, and better protecting their systems and data from cyber-attacks.

In Summary

Compliance with the UK GDPR and DPA 2018 is crucial for financial services firms. It not only helps avoid significant penalties but also builds trust with customers and protects the firm's reputation. As data protection regulations continue to evolve, firms must stay informed and adapt their practices accordingly.

By implementing robust data protection measures and fostering a culture of privacy awareness, financial services firms can navigate the complex landscape of data protection regulation and maintain compliance with both the UK GDPR and FCA requirements.

Chapter 21: Anti-Money Laundering (AML) Activities

Within the broad scope of responsibilities that a Compliance Manager handles, Anti-Money Laundering (AML) and Counter-Terrorist Financing (CTF) activities stand out as particularly crucial aspects. These activities require careful attention to ensure that businesses comply with strict AML regulatory demands. To achieve this, companies must establish and enforce clear policies and procedures that are free from any ambiguity. In this chapter, we aim to deliver a concise overview of the essential requirements involved in AML compliance. However, it's important to remember that these guidelines should be adapted to fit your firm's specific business model.

While we will not delve deeply into every detail, it is vital that your procedures align with the most current regulations and best practices in the field.

Know Your Customer (KYC) Approvals

One of the fundamental components of AML compliance is the Know Your Customer (KYC) process. This process is essential because it involves the verification of the identity and address of new clients before engaging in any transactions with them. The KYC process serves as the primary barrier against potential money laundering and terrorist financing activities.

Components of KYC

1. **Identity Verification**: Clients must provide valid identification, such as a passport or driver's license, which includes a photograph. This identification must be verified by the firm to ensure authenticity.
2. **Residential Evidence**: Clients must also provide proof of their current address to confirm their residency. This can be in the form of utility bills or bank statements.
3. **Source of Wealth and Reputation**: Beyond merely checking identity and residence, understanding a client's source of wealth, their professional background, and their general reputation is crucial. Having a comprehensive view helps verify the legitimacy of their financial activities and detect any potential risks.

The KYC process must be completed before any business is conducted with the client. However, certain exceptions may exist under specific regulations, such as the Money Laundering Regulations 2017. Additional KYC checks might be necessary for clients located in different jurisdictions, involved in high-value transactions, or those identified as Politically Exposed Persons (PEPs). Firms should be prepared with contingency plans for these particular situations.

If a firm cannot complete the KYC process to a satisfactory level or if there is doubt about a client's legitimacy, the business relationship should not continue. In such cases, any suspicions must be reported to the National Crime Agency (NCA).

Risk Management Strategies

To manage risks effectively, firms can implement several strategies, including:

- **Risk-Based Client Ratings**: Clients who fall below a particular risk threshold might have their approvals handled by administrative staff, while those who pose higher risks need to be reviewed and approved by the compliance department.
- **Compliance Oversight**: Regular audits or random checks should be conducted by the compliance team on client approvals that were initially handled by administrative staff.
- **Centralised Approvals**: Designating a specific team member or department to centralise KYC approvals can ensure greater consistency and adherence to compliance standards.

Sanctions Monitoring

The United Kingdom imposes strict sanctions lists published by HM Treasury as well as the European Union and the United Nations. These lists identify individuals and entities with whom business transactions are prohibited. Conducting comprehensive sanctions checks on all new clients is essential, as these lists are updated frequently.

Additionally, firms engaged in transactions involving US dollars must also be aware of the US sanctions regime. This regime is managed by the Office of Foreign Assets Control (OFAC) and has a far-reaching impact beyond just the United States.

Reporting Suspicious Transactions

All firms are under a legal obligation to report any suspected cases of money laundering or terrorist financing to the NCA. As part of this responsibility, firms must implement robust procedures designed to detect suspicious activities. Ensuring that all employees receive adequate training on recognising and reporting these activities is equally important.

Procedures and regular training or refresher training should be implemented so that staff are aware constitutes a suspicious and a certain level of written reminder for them to refer to should be provided along with a pro forma reporting tool. This document should include;

- person reporting the suspicion
- date suspicion reported
- dates to which the suspicion relates
- nature of suspicion
- other persons concerned in the case
- client involved
- was legal advice considered/taken (details to be included)
- whether the report was forwarded to the NCA
- if so with what justification
- date suspicion considered closed (or reported to NCA)

Whenever a report is made the Compliance Manager should always investigate and if there is any foundation to the suspicion a report to NCA should be made. NCA issues guidance about procedures to be followed in relation to reports of suspicions and these should be followed to the letter in order to avoid legal actions in the future. Tipping off is a very real occurrence and thereby procedures supplied should be followed to the letter.

Reporting Mechanism

A well-structured reporting process is crucial, and it should include:

- **Recording Details**: Every report should include detailed information such as the name of the person reporting, the date of the report, the nature of the suspicion, and the details of the parties involved.
- **Legal Consultation**: Firms should document any legal advice sought regarding the suspicion and the outcomes of such consultations.
- **Communication with the NCA**: Reports to the NCA must clearly outline the reasons and justifications for the suspicion.

The NCA provides comprehensive guidance on the reporting process, and adherence to this guidance is necessary to avoid legal issues. A significant risk during this process is the inadvertent "tipping off" of the client, which must be managed discreetly.

Details of the relevant AML Regulations can be found in Appendix 1.

Ongoing KYC Reviews

Recent regulations, such as the Money Laundering Regulations of 2017, mandate continuous monitoring and regular reviews of client records. This is to ensure the accuracy of stored information and compliance with the regulations. Over time, significant changes in a client's circumstances—such as a change in marital status, business interests, or financial conditions—can occur. Maintaining up-to-date client records is essential for comprehensive and effective KYC procedures.

Third-Party Introductions

Managing third-party introductions presents unique KYC challenges. Firms must put in place rigorous controls to validate KYC processes conducted by third parties, ensuring they meet the necessary standards. Relying on the KYC processes of other entities should not compromise the firm's own due diligence responsibilities.

In summary

Implementing effective AML and CTF measures is essential in protecting financial systems from illegal activities. Compliance Managers play a key role in ensuring that firms keep pace with evolving regulations and maintain solid, flexible procedures. Routine training, audits, and updates to systems and processes are vital components of a strong, resilient AML framework. By adhering to these standards, firms contribute significantly to safeguarding the integrity of the financial sector.

Appendices

Appendix 1: Applicable AML Regulations

The impacts of these various pieces of legislation may not directly impact on all sized firms, but it is always useful to be aware of them in case of future developments and especially if dealing with corporates or HNW clients that have overseas interests. A brief explanation follows. The key sections of this Order that are of relevance to financial services firms are noted below. ***Only those of particular relevance to financial services firms are covered.***

1. ***The Anti-Terrorism, Crime and Security Act 2001***

   Overview

   ATCSA strengthens the UK government's powers to combat terrorism, as previously
   Set out in the Terrorism Act 2000 (TACT) (see page 14), and it amends TACT in number of areas. One particular addition of note is the arrangements in sections 17 – 20 (see below)
   Designed to strengthen both the national and international anti-terrorist network. ATCSA is not aimed only at combating terrorism and also has provisions relating to other areas relevant to crime and security such as bribery, corruption and actions likely to have a detrimental effect on the UK economy.

Main elements

Firms should have systems and controls in place to ensure compliance with ATCSA;

- a failure to do so could result in a criminal offence, regulatory breaches and sanctions, and serious loss of reputation.

For further guidance on controls relating to money laundering and terrorist financing see Appendix B of the main text.

Key Sections

1 Gives effect to Schedule 1 of ATCSA which relates to the forfeiture of terrorist funds and property. Repeals sections 24–31 of TACT. Refers to Schedule 2 which amends the definition of terrorist property as initially set out in TACT.

4 - 16 Sets out procedures relating to the freezing orders that may be made if the UK Treasury reasonably believes that action is likely to take place to the detriment of the UK economy or which is likely to constitute a threat tc the life or property of a UK national or resident.

17 – 20 Provisions relating to the disclosure by public authorities (as defined under the Human Rights Act – see Appendix 3) of information relating to criminal investigations and proceedings to other authorities in the UK and overseas.

102 – 107 Provisions relating to the retention of communications data that could have an impact on a firm's record-keeping arrangements.

108 - 110 Establishes the extra territorial reach of the UK's bribery and corruption offences as set out in the:

- Prevention of Corruption Act 1906;
- Public Bodies Corrupt Practices Act 1889; and
- Prevention of Corruption Act 1916.

117 amends section 38 of TACT with the addition of section 38B which makes it an offence to fail to report information that could help to prevent terrorism.

Schedule 1 Arrangements relating to the forfeiture of terrorist cash and the handling and tracing of terrorist property. Includes a definition of terrorist cash and property. Amended slightly by section 35 of TACT 06.

Schedule 2 (part I) Amends section 38 of TACT with the addition of section 38A which gives effect to the new Schedule 6A concerning account monitoring orders.

Schedule 2 (part II) Amends Schedule 4 of TACT relating to forfeiture orders.

Schedule 2 (part III)	Amends section 21 of TACT with the addition of sections 21A, 21B. Amends Schedule 3 of TACT with the addition of Schedule 3A.
Schedule 2 (part IV)	Amends Schedule 6 of TACT

Schedule 3 additional details on freezing orders which may be implemented if the UK Treasury reasonably believes that action is likely to take place to the detriment of the UK economy or which is likely to constitute a threat to the life or property of a UK national or resident. Establishes offences relating to non-compliance with freezing orders. These offences may also be attributable to officers of bodies corporate, for example, directors and managers.

2. The Proceeds of Crime Act 2002

Overview

POCA focuses on preventing criminals from benefiting from their crimes by enhancing the ability of law enforcement agencies to seize criminal funds.

Main elements

Establishes a number of offences of which financial services firms may find themselves guilty if they fail to implement adequate money laundering arrangements. Describes how firms may be required to cooperate during the course of an investigation under POCA.

Key Sections

1 - 5 Create the Asset Recover Agency (ARA) which is a body empowered to recover profit derived from criminal activity. (Note that ARA was incorporated into the Serious and Organised Crime Agency (SOCA) and is now part of the NCA).

6 - 316 Set out the legal framework within which criminal proceeds may be confiscated.

241 Establishes that conduct undertaken overseas, that would constitute a criminal offence if undertaken in any part of the UK, is deemed to be unlawful conduct for the purposes of POCA.

327 Makes it an offence to conceal criminal property. Clarifies that the concept of concealing criminal property is very wide and includes the actions of disguising its nature, source, location, disposition, movement or ownership or any rights with respect to it. There are certain exemptions to this offence including having reported the relevant circumstances in accordance with section 338 of POCA and having received the appropriate consent under section 335 of POCA.

328 Makes it an offence for a person to enter into or become involved with an arrangement which he knows or suspects facilitates the acquisition, use, retention or control of criminal property by or on behalf of another. There are certain exemptions to this offence, including having reported the relevant circumstances in accordance with section 338 of POCA and having received the appropriate consent under section 335 of POCA.

329 Makes it an offence to acquire, use or possess criminal property. · There are certain exemptions to this offence, including having reported the relevant circumstances in accordance with section 338 of POCA and having received the appropriate consent under section 335 of POCA.

330 Makes it an offence to fail to report knowledge or a suspicion of money laundering if the following three conditions are met:

- the person has knowledge or suspects that another person is engaged in money laundering.
- the person concerned gained their knowledge or suspicion as a result of their work for a regulated firm.
- the person did not make a report of their suspicion to their firm's MLRO (or other internally

nominated person) or to another person authorized for this purpose.

There are certain exemptions to this offence – notably the fact that the person did not receive anti-money laundering training from his employer.

In considering whether an offence has been committed under this section the court will consider whether the person complied with relevant guidance such as the JMLSG Guidance Notes.

331 Makes it an offence for a nominated officer, such as an MLRO, to fail to report a suspicion of money laundering that they have received under section 330 above if three conditions are met:

- the nominated officer has knowledge or suspects that another person is engaged in money laundering.
- the person concerned gained their knowledge or suspicion as a result of a disclosure made under section 330 above.
- the person did not make a report of their suspicion to a person nominated for this purpose by SOCA (now NCA).

Failure to report is not an offence if there is an explanation for the fact that a report was not made. In considering whether an offence has been committed under this section the court will consider whether the nominated officer complied with relevant guidance such as the JMLSG Guidance Notes.

333 Establishes the offence of tipping off. The offence of tipping off is committed if a person knows or suspects that a disclosure has been made under sections 337 or 338 above and he discloses this fact in such a way that is likely to jeopardize any resultant investigation. There are certain limited exemptions.

334 Sets out the penalties for offences created under sections 327–333 (see below). 335 Defines 'appropriate consent' for the purposes of the exemptions to the offences described at sections 327–329 of POCA.

336 Sets out the circumstances in which those authorized to give 'appropriate consent' may do so. If consent is given in breach of this section an offence is committed.

337 Defines the term 'protected disclosures'. A person may lawfully disclose a suspicion or knowledge of money laundering (where otherwise disclosing the information would have been an offence), as long as the disclosure meets certain conditions including that of having been made to a constable, a customs officer or a nominated officer such as the person's MLRO. 338 Defines the term 'authorized disclosure' for the purposes of the exemptions to the offences described at sections 327–329 of POCA.

339 Sets out requirements relating to the form and manner of disclosures as per sections 330,

331, 332 and 338 of POCA.

340 Clarifies the meaning of certain terms used in POCA including those described below. Establishes that 'criminal conduct' includes conduct undertaken overseas that would constitute a criminal offence if undertaken in any part of the UK. Defines the term 'criminal property' for the purposes of POCA. Property is defined very broadly and includes money and all forms of property, real or personal, heritable or moveable, or intangible. Provides the following definition of money laundering:

– an act which:

- constitutes an offence under section 327, 328 or 329 of POCA;

- constitutes an attempt, conspiracy or incitement to commit an offence
- specified in paragraph (a);
- constitutes aiding, abetting, counselling or procuring the commission of an
- offence specified in paragraph (a); or
- would constitute an offence specified in paragraph (a), (b) or (c) if done in the United Kingdom.

Defines the terms 'constable' and 'nominated officer'.

341 Describes the various types of investigation that may take place under POCA including money-laundering investigations.

342 Makes it an offence (with certain exemptions) to prejudice an investigation under POCA.

345-346 Describe arrangements relating to production orders that may be made during an investigation under POCA.

347 Indicates that production orders may authorize entry to premises during the course of an investigation under POCA.

352 - 356 Set out arrangements in relation to search and seizure warrants that may be issued during the course of an investigation under POCA.

357-362 Set out arrangements in relation to disclosure orders that may be issued during the course of an investigation under POCA.

359 Set out the offences that may be committed in relation to disclosure orders.

363-369 Establish that financial services firms may be subject to customer information orders under POCA. Describe arrangements in relation to such customer information orders. Customer information orders require firms to disclose certain key pieces of information about a customer including:

- account number;
- full name;
- date of birth;
- evidence of identity obtained by the firm; and
- tax number.

366 Sets out the offences that may be committed in relation to customer information orders (see below).

370-376 Establish that financial services firms may be required to comply with account monitoring orders under POCA.

Describe arrangements in relation to such account monitoring orders.

Account monitoring orders require firms to provide account information to a particular law enforcement agency if certain illegal activity, including money laundering, is suspected.

There are special arrangements for making account monitoring orders relating to information held overseas.

Sch 1 Describes arrangements for the operation of the Assets Recovery Agency

Sch 2, 4 & 5 List the offences known as 'lifestyle' offences in England and Wales, Scotland and Northern Ireland respectively.

Lifestyle offences are those that would tend to indicate that a person has a 'criminal lifestyle' and may therefore be subject to the assets confiscation regime under POCA.

3.

4. The Serious Organised Crime and Police Act 2005

Overview

Law designed to strengthen the powers of the police to combat serious, organised crime.

Main elements

The body responsible for receiving notifications of suspicions of money laundering is the National Crime Agency (NCA). Firms must comply with the detailed requirements of NCA when dealing with a suspicion of money laundering. Financial services firms may be required to provide information or documents under a disclosure order to assist with a criminal investigation. Firms or individuals convicted of certain offences may find themselves subject to a financial reporting order. NCA amends certain key sections of POCA.

Key Sections

1-59 These sections establish the responsibilities, powers and general modus operandi of NCA.

60-65 Confer powers on relevant investigating authorities to make disclosure notices in relation to certain crimes. The investigating authorities referenced are the:

- Director of Public Prosecutions;
- Director of Revenue and Customs Prosecutions;
- Lord Advocate.
- The crimes covered include:
- drug trafficking;
- money laundering;
- engaging in terrorist activities.
- Disclosure notices can be made by:

- a police constable;
- an appropriately designated member of NCA; or
- an officer of Revenue and Customs.

Disclosure notices are designed to assist with investigations into crime and require persons on whom an order has been made to provide information and/or documents in accordance with the time and place requirements stipulated by the relevant investigating authority.

66 Establishes the power of the authorities to seize documents subject to a disclosure notice under warrant if these have not been produced as required.

67 Failure to comply with a disclosure notice may constitute an offence (see below).

68-70 Various other matters relating to disclosure notices, including the ways in which disclosure notices may be given.

76-81 Financial reporting orders may be made on persons found guilty of certain crimes such as:

- drug trafficking;
- money laundering;
- engaging in terrorist activities.

Financial reporting orders require the subject to disclose details of their financial affairs and supply supporting documentation. Failure to comply with a financial reporting order constitutes an offence.

95 -96 Provision relating to the strengthening of international cooperation in fighting crime.

97–109 Various amendments to POCA, including (at section 102) the removal of the troublesome Spanish bullfighter problem).

Schedules 1-4 Matters relating to the operation of NCA.

5. The Terrorism Act 2000 (as amended by the Anti-Terrorism, Crime and Security Act 2001).

Overview

TACT defines terrorism for the purposes of the UK legal system and creates the legal powers necessary to combat it.
It is the UK's primary counter-terrorism legislation.
TACT creates a number of offences related to involvement in arrangements for facilitating, raising or using funds for terrorist purposes. Specifically, it is an offence:

- Not to report a suspicion of terrorist activity where there are reasonable grounds to suspect this; and

- To take action that is likely to 'tip off' a person who is suspected of involvement in terrorism.

TACT gives law enforcement agencies the power to make account monitoring orders, similar to those introduced by POCA if it is suspected that a particular client account is being used for terrorist purposes.

TACT also lists organisations that have been proscribed, and with which firms should not consequently conduct business.

Main elements

TACT makes it an offence to facilitate terrorism in any way and as a consequence financial services firms must make sure that they have the appropriate systems and controls in place to ensure that they are not unwittingly used for this purpose.

Key Sections

1	Provides a definition of terrorism for the purposes of TACT. Amended slightly by section 34 of TACT 06.
3-13	Matters relating to proscribed organisations (suspected of involvement with terrorism). Amended by sections 21 and 22 of TACT 06 to have a more extensive reach.
14	Provides a definition of terrorist property for the purposes of TACT. This has been amended by Schedule 2 of the ATCSA.
15	Creates the offence of terrorist fund raising – see below.

16 Creates the offence of use and possession of terrorist money or property – see below.

17 & 18 Create the offence of being involved in terrorist funding arrangements – see below.

19 & 20 Creates the requirement to report a suspicion of an offence having been committed under sections 15–18 of TACT. Require such reports to be made as soon as is reasonably practical to either a constable or to an appropriately nominated person (such as the MLRO) within a financial services firm.

The duty to report only applies when a person forms a suspicion on the basis of their involvement with their trade, profession, business or employment. (By way of example, if you are travelling on public transport and suspect that a fellow passenger is carrying a bomb then you are under no legal duty to report this. However, if you are at work in a bank and suspect that one of your customers is using their account to fund terrorist activities, you have a duty to report it.)

21 Provides that it is not an offence for a person to continue their involvement with a constable (or to the relevant internal person such as the MLRO) and the constable has not forbidden their continuing involvement.

21A Addition to TACT created under the ATCSA. Creates an offence specifically covering persons working within the regulated sector for failure to report a suspicion of terrorism.

21B Addition to TACT created under the ATCSA. Establishes 'protected disclosure' requirements specifically for the regulated sector whereby an employee of a regulated sector firm may report a suspicion of terrorist activity to a constable or to a 'nominated officer' appointed by their employer.

22 Sets out the penalties for an offence under sections 15 – 18 of TACT – see below.

24-31 These sections previously set out the powers of forfeiture created under TACT in relation to money or property belonging to a person convicted under sections 15 – 18. However, they have ceased to have effect under section 1.4 of the ATCSA.

37 Gives effect to Schedule 5 of TACT which sets out the powers of a constable to search premises and seize material as part of a terrorist investigation. Amended and strengthened by section 26 of TACT 06.

38	Gives effect to Schedule 6 of TACT which sets out the powers of a constable to obtain financial information about the clients of a financial institution. Such information includes evidence of a person's identity obtained for KYC purposes and the date on which the relationship with the financial institution began or ended.
38A	Addition to TACT created under the ATCSA. Gives effect to the new Schedule 6A concerning account monitoring orders.
38B	Addition to TACT created under the ATCSA. Makes it an offence to fail to disclose certain information about terrorism.
39	Creates the offences of 'tipping off' a person subject to a terrorist investigation and/or interfering with material likely to be relevant to such an investigation.
63	Establishes the extraterritorial reach of TACT by stating that if an act constituting an offence under TACT is committed outside the UK, the person who commits it shall still be deemed to have committed an offence for the purposes of TACT.
64	Amends the Extradition Act 1989 to cover offences under sections 15 – 18 of TACT (now repealed and incorporated into the Extradition Act 2003).
Schedule 2	Lists the organisations proscribed under TACT.

Schedule 3A	Addition to TACT created under the ATCSA. Defines regulated sector businesses and supervisory authorities (including the *FCA*) for the purposes of TACT.
Schedule 4	Procedures and arrangements relating to forfeiture orders made under TACT. Amended by the ATCSA.
Schedule 5	See section 37 above – terrorist investigations.
Schedule 6	See section 38 above – provision of financial information during the course of an investigation into terrorism. Amended by Schedule 2 Part IV of the ATCSA.
Schedule 6A	Addition to TACT created under the ATCSA. Procedures relating to Account Monitoring Orders which may be made specifically against financial services institutions for the purposes of tracing suspected terrorist cash property.

6. The Terrorism Act 2006

Overview

Enacted in order to further strengthen the government's powers to combat the threat of international terrorism.

Main elements

See comments for previous section - TACT 00.

Key Sections

21 Amends section 3 of TACT 00 to increase the scope of activities that may lead to an organisation being proscribed.

22 Amends section 3 of TACT 00 to cover name changes of proscribed organisations.

26 Amends Schedule 5 Part I of TACT 00 to increase powers relating to searches for the purposes of terrorist investigations.

34 Slight amendment to the definition of terrorism set out in section 1 of TACT 00.

35 Slight amendment to Schedule 1 of the ATCSA concerning the amount of time that seized terrorist cash may be held.

7. The Terrorism (United Nations Measures) Order 2006

Overview

Prohibits terrorist financing and the provision of financial services to terrorists.

Allows the Treasury to freeze the funds/ accounts of suspected terrorists.

Main elements

The asset freezing provisions introduced under the Terrorism Order may result in liquidity problems – assets that are due to be paid to a third party may be frozen and consequently, additional funds will need to be made available to meet the delivery obligations.

Firms that do not have adequate controls in place to counter their being used to provide financial services to terrorists may find themselves guilty of an offence under the Terrorism Order.

Key Sections

2 Provides definition for key terms used in the Terrorism Order.

3 & 4 Relate to the designation of individuals for the purposes of this Order. A person may be designated either by a decision of the EU Council or by a direction of the UK Treasury. The Treasury may designate persons in a number of circumstances – if it suspects that a person is:

- involved with terrorism;
- subject to an EU Council decision relating to this area;
- owned or controlled, either directly or indirectly, by a designated person;

- acting on behalf of a designated person.

5 Requires the Treasury, among other things, to publicize its decision to designate a person under this Order.

6 Makes it an offence to disclose information about the Treasury's decision to designate a person under this Order where this information has only been made available to certain persons.

7 Makes it an offence for a person to deal with funds or other economic resources belonging to a person designated under this Order. Accounts in which such funds or economic resources are held are deemed 'frozen accounts' for the purposes of this Order. For the purposes of this Order, the definition of 'to deal with' is very wide and covers most if not all involvement that a financial services firm could have with a designated person. A person may only deal with such funds legal under the authority of a licence issued by the Treasury under article 11 of this Order.

8 Makes it an offence to make funds, economic resources or financial services available, directly or indirectly, to or for the benefit of a person designated under this order. The restrictions in this section may only be lawfully breached with the authority of licence issued by the Treasury under article 11 of this Order.

10 Makes it an offence to breach, or assist another person in breaching, requirements under sections 7 and 8 of this Order.

11	Covers the Treasury's authority to grant a licence for lawfully engaging in activities that would otherwise be illegal under sections 7 and 8 of this Order.
13	Sets out the penalties that may be imposed for breaching this Order. Provides that where a body corporate has been found guilty of an offence under this Order, then its directors, managers and other staff may also be guilty of an offence.
Schedule 1.1	Requires the Treasury to cooperate fully with any national or international investigation regarding a person designated under this Order.
Schedule 1.2	Makes it an offence for a financial institution to fail to inform the Treasury of knowledge or a suspicion that a designated person has committed an offence under sections 6, 7, 8, 10 or 11 of this Order where that person is or has been a customer of the firm, or the firm has otherwise had involvement with them, since the implementation of the Terrorism (United Nations Measures) Order 2001.
Schedule 1.3	Gives authority to the Treasury to require information and documents to be made available to it in cases in which terrorism is suspected.

Schedule 1.4 Sets out the penalties for failing to provide information to the Treasury during a terrorism investigation and for failing to cooperate with Treasury investigations into terrorism.

8. Trade and Financial Sanctions Legislation

Overview

Trade and financial sanctions legislation is aimed at preventing the UK's financial system from being used by criminal or corrupt regimes, organisations or persons or for facilitating undesirable activities such as terrorism and arms dealing. The regime is the overall responsibility of the Foreign and Commonwealth Office with the financial sanctions regime being operated by the Asset Freezing Unit of HM Treasury and the trade sanctions regime being operated by the Department for Business, Enterprise and Regulatory Reform.

New sanctions are accompanied by a statutory instrument so that they are legally enforceable and details are published on the Treasury's website. This should be checked regularly by Compliance as firms must not conduct any trades in breach of financial sanctions legislation.

Appendix 2: Bribery Act 2010

Many authorised firms are still wondering about the best way to implement the Bribery Act and what it means to them as a business and a trading company that uses and provides corporate entertainment. Though mostly common sense and good business practice, whenever a legislative wrapper is placed around guidance, people are wary of not falling foul of the new law.

Our aim is to provide you with a brief insight into what can be a complex area, and give you contact details of specialists who can help and assist you with your strategy, governance and operational needs.

Introduction

Now part of British Law, the *Bribery Act 2010* (The Act) reforms criminal law to provide a new, modern and comprehensive scheme of bribery offences as never before understood, that will enable courts and prosecutors to respond more effectively to bribery at home or abroad.

The Act applies to all persons individual and corporate making it an offence to; a) Bribe another person; or b) to be in receipt of a bribe from another person.

The Scope of the Act

The Act deals with bribery which is defined as giving someone a financial or other advantage to encourage that person to perform their function or activities improperly, or to reward that person for having already done so.

Surprisingly for some, The Act is not concerned with other offences such as fraud, theft or offences under the Companies Acts, but anyone who facilitates the movement of the proceeds of bribery also commits money laundering offences.

How could my company become liable?

Your company could become liable very easily through lack of systems and controls to prevent bribery or insufficient checks to ensure that it has not occurred. Commercial companies that seek to generate new business or maintain an existing business channel, domestic or foreign, is faced with a hugely competitive environment, and the people who are in a position to grant valuable business contracts often realise that they are in a position to demand significant benefits or favours from anybody seeking their business.

Over many years, the practice of bribing people in influential positions becomes such a well-practiced habit that in so many areas it is hardly considered to be unusual. Many companies that conduct business in these areas have become used to building such up-front costs into their tendering processes.

However, if a responsible officer of your company commits such an offence now, or they knowingly allow it to carry on, then a bribery offence is committed, and the criminal acts will be attributed to the company. The liability is fully extended to any situation where an agent, employee or intermediary pays a bribe to get business, keep business or obtain a business advantage.

If your company has failed to take the necessary steps to implement adequate procedures to prevent bribery, you will be liable for their actions.

Additionally, under FSMA section 206(1) *'If the FCA considers that an authorised person has contravened a requirement imposed on him by or under this Act … it may impose on him a penalty, in respect of the contravention, of such amount as it considers appropriate"* and the firm can be fined for breaches of Principle 3 of the *FCA's* Principles for Businesses; *"A firm must take reasonable care to organise and control its affairs responsibly and effectively, with adequate risk management systems"* and Rule SYSC 3.2.6 R of the FCA's Senior Management Arrangements, Systems and Controls Handbook *"A firm must take reasonable care to establish and maintain effective systems and controls for compliance with applicable requirements and standards under the regulatory system and for countering the risk that the firm might be used to further financial crime."*.

SYSC 4.1.1R (For Common Platform Firms) states *"A firm must have robust governance arrangements, which include a clear organisational structure with well defined, transparent and consistent lines of responsibility, effective processes to identify, manage, monitor and report the risks it is or might be exposed to, and internal control mechanisms, including sound administrative and accounting procedures and effective control and safeguard arrangements for information processing systems"*

How do I implement sufficiently adequate procedures?

Initially you need to accurately assess what bribery risks you might face. If you are a UK financial services company you have probably already undertaken a Risk Based Assessment (RBA), as part of your compliance process, but if you are a commercial organisation, you may not have undertaken such an exercise and could find that you need professional assistance to construct an accurate assessment!

Having accurately conducted your RBA, you need to consider the following elements to create an effective compliance regime to prevent bribery.

- Proportionality:
- High-Level Commitment:
- Risk Assessment:
- Due Diligence:
- Internal Communication:

- Regular Monitoring and Review

Two Most Asked Questions;

Can I still provide hospitality? Can I make facilitation payments?

Yes, you can still provide business hospitality, as long as it is reasonable and proportionate in all the circumstances. As the Justice Minister, Kenneth Clark has said;

'... Taking customers to Twickenham is normal...but if you took them for a Caribbean cruise with their wife, that's different. It is normal business hospitality to get to know your customers better. No one is going to call that dishonest...'

However, in too many circumstances, the demands of hospitality have become a cover-all for expenditure that reaches such a volume that it cannot be described as anything other than a bribe, and it is this degree of proportionality which will be measured in the future.

Secondly; No, facilitation payments will not be permitted. Unlike the US law, such payments are still defined as bribes in UK law and will be dealt with as such.

What should I be doing to ensure that I am fully compliant with the law?

You must complete a full review of your business risk areas and establish where you believe you are at the greatest risk from bribery.

Then, with this knowledge and having established your full RBA, you should implement a full compliance review, with a view to introducing a compliance policy document and implementing your internal training needs. This will then protect you from internal or external allegations that you have been negligent in preventing bribery in your organisation.

How can we help you?

Ensuring your firm is prepared for every variable takes expertise and guidance. Compliance Consultant will help you manage your risks, strengthen your compliance programme, and achieve transparency and control to meet and surpass the requirements of the *Bribery Act 2010.*

Protecting your firm and building effective systems and controls requires risk specialists with a deep understanding of the issues you are facing. In addition, our consultants can assist you in delivering your programme to your directors, staff and agents – this can also include your contractors and suppliers if this is appropriate.

Contact us today and let our experts demonstrate their knowledge and skills to drive your regulatory processes by providing you with a review of your current anti-bribery policies.

About The Author

Lee Werrell Chartered FCSI is a UK regulatory Compliance Specialist Consultant who has spent over 35 years working in the financial services arena from IFAs through to international banks. He has held many senior management positions and is known as a speaker and critically, can take FCA rules and interpret them for the benefits of the organisations he works for.

About Compliance Consultant

At ***Compliance Consultant*** we know and appreciate the need for good governance, best practice adoption and delivering coherent strategies for our clients in the complex and fluid world of financial regulation. Working with financial services companies, helping to manage their compliance and other risks so they can control their exposure, train their staff, implement regulatory change and execute their strategy. This then allows them to concentrate on their core business, become stronger through better governance, greater efficiency and increasing profitability.

We have been in business since 2000 and are a small, but perfectly formed niche consultancy. Established to serve the SME community of advisory firms in Governance, Risk & Compliance. we cover all areas of financial services from Stockbrokers to banks, pawn brokers to mortgage advisors. Just ask us first and save money on your compliance support. Retainer packages available.

Call Compliance Consultant on 0800 689 0190 or Int +44 (0)207 097 1434.

Email

info@complianceconsultant.org

Printed in Dunstable, United Kingdom

85632762R00198